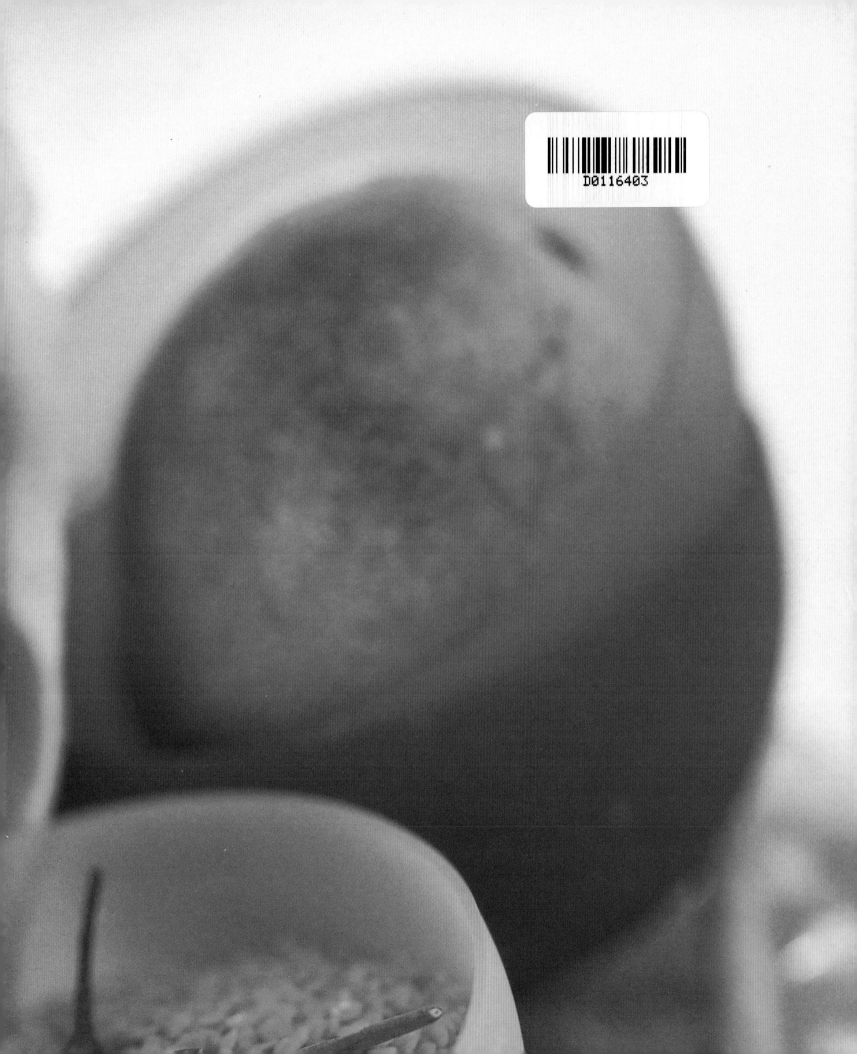

complete
indian
cooking

complete

indian

cooking

hamlyn

First published in the U.K. in 1998 by
Hamlyn a division of Octopus Publishing Group Limited
2–4 Heron Quays, London E14 4JP

This edition published 2001

Copyright © 1998, 2000, 2001 Octopus Publishing Group Ltd

ISBN 0 600 60609 0

Printed in Hong Kong

A CIP catalogue record for this book is available from the British
Library

NOTES

Both metric and imperial measurements have been given in all
recipes. Use one set of measurements only, and not a mixture of
both.

Standard level spoon measurements are used in all recipes.
1 tablespoon = one 15 ml spoon
1 teaspoon = one 5 ml spoon

Eggs should be medium to large unless otherwise stated.
The Department of Health advises that eggs should not be
consumed raw. This book contains dishes made with raw or
lightly cooked eggs. It is prudent for more vulnerable people such
as pregnant and nursing mothers, invalids, the elderly, babies and
young children to avoid uncooked or lightly cooked dishes made
with eggs. Once prepared, these dishes should be kept refrigerated
and used promptly.

Meat and poultry should be cooked thoroughly. To test if poultry
is cooked, pierce the flesh through the thickest part with a skewer
or fork — the juices should run clear, never pink or red. Do not
re-freeze poultry that has been frozen previously and thawed.
Do not re-freeze a cooked dish that has been frozen previously.

Milk should be full fat unless otherwise stated.

Nut and Nut Derivatives
This book includes dishes made with nuts and nut derivatives. It
is advisable for customers with known allergic reactions to nuts
and nut derivatives and those who may be potentially vulnerable
to these allergies, such as pregnant and nursing mothers, invalids,
the elderly, babies and children to avoid dishes made with nuts
and nut oils. It is also prudent to check the labels of pre-prepared
ingredients for the possible inclusion of nut derivatives.

Pepper should be freshly ground black pepper unless otherwise
stated.

Fresh herbs should be used, unless otherwise stated. If
unavailable, use dried herbs as an alternative, but halve the
quantities stated.

Measurements for canned food have been given as a standard
metric equivalent.

Ovens should be pre-heated to the specified temperature — if
using a fan-assisted oven, follow the manufacturer's instructions
for adjusting the time and the temperature.

Vegetarians should look for the 'V' symbol on a cheese to ensure it
is made with vegetarian rennet. There are vegetarian forms of
Parmesan, feta, Cheddar, Cheshire, Red Leicester, dolcelatte and
many goats' cheeses, among others.

Contents

Introduction

Indian cookery is not, in fact, the cuisine of a single nationality. It is, rather, the collective name given to the combination of different cuisines from many different countries.

India is a vast sub-continent, divided from the rest of Asia by the Himalayas. It is about the same size as all the countries of Europe put together, and has been home to an astonishing diversity of different peoples, speaking some 14 major languages and about 100 dialects. It is hardly surprising, then, that its cuisine should be correspondingly varied.

The influence of many different cultures, including those of the Moguls, Portuguese, Persians and British, have, over the years, given rise to many new ideas in Indian cuisine. Each region has its own particular cooking traditions, based on its specific climate and soil. The various culinary features of each region combine to lend variety, excitement and character to Indian cookery as a whole.

As a general rule, food tends to be hotter the further south you go. In more detail, the different regions can be characterized as follows.

Northern India

The Punjabi and Kashmiri styles of cooking come from the northern region of India. The north of the country is famous for its subtly spiced cooking, which owes much to the sohistication of the cooks at the luxurious courts of the Mughal emperors, who conquered northern India from Persia.

The Punjabis have the reputation of being gourmets and the best cooks in the country. The Punjab is particularly famous for its tandoori cooking and for many of its sweetmeats. Punjabis are keen wheat eaters, which they tend to consume in preference to rice.

Influenced by the Mughals, Kashmiri cooking is known for its meat cuisine. As a result, the curries that are produced in this area, which are made without any thickening agents such as onion and garlic, are close to perfection.

Ghee – clarified butter – is the most commonly used cooking fat throughout the northern part of India.

Southern India

The southern region of India is the stronghold of the Hindus. The Brahmins – who were the monitors of the Hindu faith and its temples – taught non-violence, or *ahimsa*, and thus advocated not eating meat. They declared the cow a sacred animal, which their followers were prohibited from eating.

The staple foods in the south of India are therefore vegetables and rice. Mustard oil is generally used as the cooking medium, and coconut, coconut milk and tamarind are used in many of the local recipes. Curries from this part of India, which include the fierce vindaloo curries, are thin and fiery, using plenty of chillies.

"... the fierce vindaloo curries are thin and fiery, using plenty of chillies."

sophisticated way of cooking. The Mughals ate meat, including the cow which was sacred for the Hindus, and their culinary influence is particularly evident in the regional meat dishes.

Eastern India

Eastern India – which encompasses Bengal and Bihar – is surrounded by rivers and seas. It is hardly surprising, therefore, that fish – which is both plentiful and inexpensive – should be such an important part of the local diet. Mustard oil is used as the principal cooking medium, which gives a slightly sweet flavour. Foods are spiced with mustard, cumin, anise and fenugreek seeds. The easterners are known for their delicious sweetmeats and savouries.

Western India

The cuisine of western India comes principally from Goa and Bombay. Goan food tends to be hot and spicy and uses a lot of coconut milk, vinegar and tamarind juice. Dishes are cooked very slowly for a long time, which gives them a wonderfully rich flavour. Bombay is famed for its delicious fruit ice-creams and for its refreshing cold drinks, made with fruit juices and yogurt, which are known as sharbats.

Central India

The cuisine from the central area of India is dominated by the Mughal influence, and is an especially refined and

Curries

Ask anyone in the West what first springs to mind when they think of Indian food and they are almost certain to say curry. The word curry is thought to come from the Tamil, or southern Indian, word *kari*, which means sauce, or from *karhai*, which is a commonly used Indian cooking vessel. Most curry sauces are characteristically aromatic, and are redolent of the rich blend of spices that are combined in them.

In India, the various ingredients that are used to make a curry depend largely on the taste of the individual who is preparing the dish. It is usual for all the ingredients, including spices, roots and seeds, to be ground separately into a paste with a little water on what is known as a 'curry stone'. Once it has been made, a good curry powder will keep for years.

While there are many different flavours which recur frequently in curry making, such as coconut, ginger, onions and tamarind, no dish can be called a curry if it does not contain a selection of spices. Many different spices are used in curries, all of them with a distinctive flavour, which is why there are so many different curries in India, for there is almost no limit to the possible combinations of spices.

Weights and measures are seldom used by Indian chefs. Much depends on the particular skill and judgement of the cook to produce the perfect aromatic curry, which must be neither too hot, nor too bland. The secret lies in finding the right proportions, which is something that can only come from experience. The traditional Indian culinary artiste guesses the quantities and gets perfect results every time.

Curry making owes a great deal to trial and error and you, too, can experiment with the quantities of spices you use. Indian chefs would never be limited by recipes, and these are only a guide. Use smaller quantities of these ingredients to start with, particularly if you are not yet used to Indian flavours, but always use them in the correct proportions, as instructed in the recipe.

Curry is the name given to a large group of dishes, produced in a number of different ways and with a wide range of different flavours. Some of these are wet; some dry; some are hot; some mild; some creamy; and some fruity; The range of different dishes is legendary.

Spices

Indians are skilled in using and blending spices – a skill that they have fortunately never lost over the years, in spite of their being influenced by so many other countries. Spices are dried aromatic parts of plants, including the seeds, leaves, roots and bark. Their principal use is to flavour food.

The majority of spices are grown in tropical countries, though they are believed also to have been used in the eastern Mediterranean for some 5,000 years. The appeal of exotic spices used to be so great that they were once believed to be a gift worthy of royalty, and long hazardous journeys were undertaken in order to bring them back from far-away places such as China, Indonesia and, of course, India.

It is a commonly held belief in India that spicy and exotic food makes the people who eat it more virile. Lord Krishna of India, for example, is said to have had some 16,000 wives, the implication being that he acquired his virility from the food he ate.

But it is wrong to think that Indian food should always be hot. Very hot food burns the palate, the skin on the tongue and has a tendency to upset the tummy, particularly when eaten by someone who is unaccustomed to spicy food. Not all the spices that are used in India are hot. It is only the chillies and pepper that give a kick.

Dry-frying, or roasting spices brings out their distinctive flavours. It is usual in Indian cooking to dry-fry several whole spices at once, depending on what you will need in the recipe. Use a heavy-based frying pan, put all the spices in an even layer into the pan and set over a moderate heat. Stir-fry the spices for about 5 minutes until they are a shade or two darker and beginning to give off a delicious aroma. Allow the spices to cool, then grind them with a pestle and mortar. An electric coffee grinder, kept specially for the purpose, makes grinding whole spices much easier.

Vegetarian food

India has, for a long time, been regarded as the centre of the vegetarian world. One reason for this may be because Hindus are forbidden by their religion to eat meat. In general, Indians are a peaceful people and have a great abhorrence for killing anything, including animals. Another cause could be that the economic reasons, vegetables being much less expensive than meat.

Ingredients

It is important always to use the very best ingredients possible. Where poultry, meat and vegetables are concerned, the western cook is at an immediate advantage, since the quality is usually better than that available to his or her eastern counterpart.

But when it comes to the selection of Indian ingredients, it is important to take the utmost care. Unless you use the same ingredients as those that are used in India, you cannot expect to produce the same results.

most commonly used for Indian food is Patna or, as the native cook in India calls it, 'table rice'. It comes in various grades and qualities and is available either polished or unpolished. The best results will be obtained using the finest grade of unpolished Patna rice.

Basmati rice is another good Indian rice. It has small but long grains and a distinctive flavour. It is available in both brown and white versions.

This applies, in particular, to spices, which add a distinctive flavour and colour.

Specialist Indian ingredients are now easily available from many supermarkets and Indian food stores. Because so many Indian people now live abroad and because of the proliferation of Indian restaurants, Indian food is enjoying a great revival in popularity and most major cities have speciality Indian shops and food stores. Just a look round these shops yields a fascinating glimpse into the rich diversity of Indian culture.

Another excellent source of Indian ingredients is your nearest large supermarket. People have become very interested in Indian food, with the result that a good range of ingredients is now available. You will find special features throughout this book which supply detailed information about specialist Indian ingredients.

Storecupboard ingredients

There are many ingredients that you will find in your storecupboard and which will come in useful for Indian cookery. Some of these are included below.

Rice
Rice is highly nutritious and is an important accompaniment to curries. The particular type of rice

Fat
The fat most commonly used in India is ghee, which is clarified butter – either buffalo or cow. Clarified means that all the milk solids have been removed. Ghee does not need to be refrigerated and is ideal for Indian cooking techniques, as it can be heated to a high temperature without burning.

Ghee was first developed in northern India, probably by nomadic peoples who had no regular crops of oil-rich foods and were in need of an easily transportable cooking fat. When it is properly made, it is absolutely free from moisture and impurities, and will neither splutter, nor burn or blacken. It has a particularly rich, nutty flavour.

In India, the best ghee is homemade. When it is sold in Indian markets it is often adulterated with nut oil and other fats. But pure ghee is expensive and therefore, out of the reach of many ordinary people. Other fats, such as sesame oil, mustard oil, coconut oil and cottonseed oil, are commonly used instead and virtually any neutral-flavoured vegetable oil can be used. Sunflower and groundnut oil are good all-purpose oils.

Ghee is available in this country from some supermarkets and specialist Indian foodstores. It is sold in tins and keeps well for up to two or three months in the refrigerator.

Yogurt

Yogurt is often used to add a sharp creaminess to Indian curries. Use a natural yogurt, preferably a thin tart-flavoured variety rather then the milder, creamier Greek type. If you use a 'set' yogurt, always stir it a little to break up the 'setting' before adding it to the curry or serving it as an accompaniment.

Cooking utensils

Indian food can be cooked using all the usual utensils that you have in your kitchen, and you need very few – if any – special pieces of equipment. Cooking is often done using one utensil called a *karhai*, which is similar to the Chinese wok, its purpose being to use as little oil as possible. A saucepan or a heavy-based frying pan will usually do just as well.

Fresh stock recipes

You will find it useful to have these basic recipes to hand as they are required throughout the book. A good stock is both easy and inexpensive to make, with only a few basic ingredients. A fresh aromatic broth is far superior to commercial stock cubes and, once it is made, a good stock can be frozen in small batches in plastic tubs or ice cube trays and used as required.

A few basic rules are necessary when making stock.
• Stock should always simmer extremely gently, or it will evaporate too quickly and become cloudy.
• Never add salt to the stock as simmering will reduce it

Coconut milk

Coconut milk is essential in Indian cookery. It can be made using either desiccated or fresh coconut, which gives a richer, more mellow flavour and a creamier consistency.

There is no need, nowadays and in this part of the world, to extract coconut milk from the coconut. Canned coconut milk is readily available in many supermarkets and Indian foodstores. It is unsweetened and works extremely well.

Coconut milk powder is also available, which needs to be mixed with water to produce coconut milk. Do this according to the packet instructions and add more or less water according to how thick or thin you want it to be.

Spices

A good selection of spices is a must. The most widely used of these include aniseed, asafoetida, black onion seeds, cardamom, chillies, cinnamon, cloves, coriander seeds, cumin, fennel seeds, fenugreek, mustard seeds, nutmeg, saffron and turmeric.

It is best to keep only small quantities of frequently used spices in the kitchen, and to store them in a cool, dry place. Use them within six months of buying, as a stale spice has very little to offer any curry.

Fish stock

You should be able to get the bones for this stock from the fishmonger, but avoid the bones of oily fish. It is important that this stock does not boil as it will become very cloudy.

• Place 1½ kg/3 lb fish trimmings and 1 onion, sliced, the white part of 1 small leek, 1 celery stick, sliced, 1 bay leaf, 6 parsley stalks, 10 whole peppercorns and 475 ml/16 fl oz of dry white wine into a large pot. Cover with 1.8 litres/3 pints cold water.
• Bring slowly to just below boiling point and simmer for 20 minutes, removing any scum from the surface. Strain the stock through a muslin-lined sieve and leave to cool before refrigerating.

Makes 1.8 litres/3 pints
Preparation time: *10 minutes*
Cooking time: *20 minutes*

and concentrate the flavour. This will affect the overall flavour of the finished dish.
• Any scum that rises to the surface should be removed as it will spoil the colour and flavour of the final stock.
• Avoid any floury root vegetables as these will cause the stock to become cloudy.

Chicken stock

The following recipe is light and delicately flavoured.

• Chop a cooked chicken carcass into 3 or 4 pieces and place it in a large pot with the raw giblets and trimmings, 1 onion roughly chopped, 2 large carrots roughly chopped, 1 celery stalk roughly chopped, 1 bay leaf, a few parsley stalks lightly crushed, and 1 sprig of thyme. Add 1.8 litres/3 pints of cold water.
• Bring this to the boil, removing any scum from the surface. Lower the heat and simmer for 2–2½ hours. Strain the stock through a muslin-lined sieve and leave to cool completely before refrigerating.

Makes 1 litre/1¾ pints
Preparation time: *5–10 minutes*
Cooking time: *about 1½ hours*

Vegetable stock

This simple recipe makes a well-flavoured vegetable stock. You can ring the changes according to which vegetables are in season.

• Place 500 g/1 lb chopped mixed vegetables such as carrots, leeks, celery, onion or mushrooms in a large saucepan. Add 1 garlic clove, 6 peppercorns, and 1 bouquet garni (2 parsley sprigs, 2 thyme sprigs and 1 bay leaf). Cover with 1.2 litres/2 pints water.
• Bring to the boil and simmer gently for 30 minutes, skimming the surface of the stock, when necessary. Strain the stock and allow to cool completely before refrigerating.

Makes 1 litre/1¾ pints
Preparation time: *5–10 minutes*
Cooking time: *about 45 minutes*

Cook's tools

There are so many good things and good people in India,
that what they eat is no mean study,
for food often maketh man.

Lt.Gen. Sir George MacMunn,
K.C.B., K.C.S.I., D.S.O.

In Indian cooking, kitchen tools are relatively basic, and you will probably already have most of the equipment you need in your kitchen.

Colander

The colander is used for separating liquids from solids, and for draining and rinsing food. Although colanders come in many different shapes and sizes, they are basically a container with holes and are usually made of plastic or stainless steel. A colander is ideal for rinsing food and for draining rice and vegetables.

Grater

Graters come in either a box shape or a single flat sheet. Both shapes have perforations which perform different functions. The fine holes are for grating spices and rind, the medium and large holes are for grating cheese and vegetables. Graters are generally made of stainless steel, as it is hard-wearing and does not rust. If you have a flat sheet grater, ensure that the grater is properly balanced when grating, as this sort does have a tendency to slip.

Mixing bowl

A mixing bowl should be wide enough to allow mixtures to be beaten or gently folded. The bowl should be rested on a grip stand to prevent it slipping.

Rolling pin

A rolling pin is used for rolling out bread dough or pastry to a smooth, flat, even sheet. It should be heavy so that it – rather than you – does the work. A rolling pin can be made of wood, plastic, nylon or marble, and should be wide and well balanced. When rolling out any mixture, use flour to stop the mixture sticking to the pin. Wipe the rolling pin clean before storing it.

Chopping board

As its name suggests, the chopping board is a surface that is used for chopping food including meat, vegetables and fruit. It should be made from a material that is soft enough not to blunt a knife, but hard enough to resist splintering. Boards are generally made of wood, or a synthetic material. Wooden boards require sanding and oiling in order to maintain them. Some cooks prefer a synthetic material, such as plastic, as it is easier to keep clean and sterile. Whichever material you choose, your board should be as large as you have room for on your work surface.

Pestle and mortar

A pestle and mortar are essentially a grinder with a bowl, and is one of the earliest grinding tools known to man. Such a utensil has been in use for thousands of years for grinding herbs and spices, and is still widely used today as it is so efficient. Pestles and mortars come in many different sizes, according to needs, and can be made of ceramic, stone, wood or metal. The insides of the bowl should be rough and unglazed.

Knives (chopping, paring)

A good cook is not equipped without a set of good kitchen knives. Knives should always be well maintained, cleaned, thoroughly dried, and sharpened regularly.

Chopping knife: A heavy, wide-blade knife, this is ideal for chopping all vegetables and other ingredients. It is also good for flattening thinly sliced meats, and transferring ingredients from the board to the pan.

Paring knife: This is a small, sharp knife, which is used for trimming and peeling fruit and vegetables.

Soups and
Starters

Fish and Coconut Soup

500 g/1 lb monkfish or halibut fillet, skinned and cubed

25 g/1 oz desiccated coconut

6 shallots

6 almonds, blanched

2 garlic cloves, peeled

2.5 cm/1 inch piece of fresh root ginger, peeled and sliced

2 blades of lemon grass, trimmed

2–3 teaspoons turmeric

3 tablespoons oil

1 fresh red chilli, deseeded and sliced

salt

fresh coriander leaves, to garnish

Coconut milk

300 g/11 oz desiccated coconut

750 ml/1¼ pints boiling water

Coconut cream

300 g/11 oz desiccated coconut

750 ml/1¼ pints boiling water

make the coconut milk by placing the desiccated coconut and boiling water in a blender or food processor, and working for 20 seconds. Pour into a bowl and leave to cool to blood temperature. Strain into a clean bowl or jug.

repeat the above process to make the coconut cream, leaving the strained liquid to stand. When the cream rises to the top of the milk, skim it off – this is the coconut cream.

sprinkle the fish with salt. Place the coconut in a wok and heat gently until it is golden and crisp. Remove from the wok and pound until oily. Set aside.

purée the shallots, almonds, garlic, ginger and 6 cm/2½ inches from the root end of the lemon grass (reserving the remainder) in a blender or food processor. Add the turmeric.

heat the oil in a wok or saucepan and fry the puréed mixture for a few minutes. Add the coconut milk and bring to the boil, stirring constantly. Stir in the fish, chilli and the remaining lemon grass. Cook over a gentle heat for about 5 minutes.

stir in the pounded coconut and cook for a further 5 minutes. Remove the blades of lemon grass and stir in the coconut cream. Serve hot, garnished with coriander.

Serves 4
Preparation time: *25 minutes*
Cooking time: *15–20 minutes*

Spiced Chicken Soup

1.5 litres/2½ pints water
1 x 1.25 kg/2½ lb chicken, quartered
4 uncooked king prawns
2 macadamia nuts, chopped
4 shallots, chopped
2 garlic cloves, crushed
2 teaspoons grated fresh root ginger
pinch of turmeric
pinch of chilli powder
vegetable oil for shallow-frying
1 tablespoon light soy sauce
75 g/3 oz bean sprouts
1 potato, peeled and thinly sliced
salt and freshly ground black pepper

put the water in a large saucepan and bring to the boil. Add the chicken and prawns with a little seasoning, then cover and simmer gently for 40 minutes. Strain, reserving 1.2 litres/2 pints of the liquid. Shred the meat from the chicken and peel and chop the prawns.

blend the macadamias, shallots, garlic and ginger to a purée in a blender or food processor. Add the turmeric and chilli powder and mix well. Alternatively, pound in a mortar.

heat 2 tablespoons of oil in a saucepan, add the spice paste and fry for a few seconds. Stir in 300 ml/½ pint of the reserved liquid, the soy sauce, chicken and prawns. Simmer for 10 minutes. Add the remaining liquid and simmer for a further 10 minutes. Add the bean sprouts and cook for 3 minutes.

fry the potato slices in some hot oil, while the soup is cooking, until golden and crisp. Remove and drain on absorbent kitchen paper. Serve the hot soup garnished with the fried potato.

Serves 4–6
Preparation time: *20 minutes*
Cooking time: *1¼ hours*

clipboard: The macadamia nut is the fruit of an Australian tree, which has a flavour reminiscent of coconut. It is often used in curries in Indian cookery.

Indian Split Pea Soup

This chilled soup is easy to make and is a deliciously refreshing soup for a hot summer's day. It looks pretty garnished with cucumber, spring onions and mint.

250 g/8 oz yellow split peas
1.3 litres/2¼ pints water
½ teaspoon turmeric
2 tablespoons lemon juice
1 fresh green chilli, deseeded and finely chopped
1 teaspoon ground cumin
1 teaspoon ground coriander seeds
½ small cucumber
3 spring onions
75 ml/3 fl oz natural yogurt
salt and freshly ground black pepper
fresh mint leaves, to garnish

pick over the yellow split peas to remove any grit and then wash under running cold water and drain them in a colander.

place the drained split peas in a large saucepan with the water and turmeric and bring to the boil. Reduce the heat and cover the pan. Simmer very gently for 1¼–1½ hours until cooked and tender. Remove from the heat.

tip the split peas and their liquid into a large blender or food processor. Add the lemon juice, seasoning, chilli, cumin and coriander seeds and blend until smooth. If the soup is a little too thick, thin it down with water or more lemon juice. Transfer to a serving bowl and refrigerate until required.

dice the cucumber and slice the spring onions just before serving. Swirl the yogurt into the chilled soup and serve garnished with the cucumber, spring onions and mint.

Serves 4
Preparation time: *20 minutes*
Cooking time: *1¼–1½ hours*

Spiced Pea Soup

This creamy soup has a mild spicy flavour, thanks to the addition of ginger, cumin, coriander and chilli. It is a delicate green colour, garnished with fresh coriander leaves.

25 g/1 oz ghee or 1 tablespoon vegetable oil
1 large onion, coarsely chopped
2 garlic cloves, chopped
1 small potato, diced
2.5 cm/1 inch piece of fresh root ginger, peeled and sliced
1 teaspoon ground cumin seeds
1 teaspoon ground coriander seeds
900 ml/1½ pints Vegetable Stock (see page 11)
250 g/8 oz fresh or frozen peas
1 fresh green chilli, chopped
300 ml/½ pint single cream
salt and freshly ground black pepper
fresh coriander leaves, to garnish

heat the ghee or oil in a large heavy-bottomed saucepan and fry the onion and garlic gently for about 5 minutes, until soft and golden.

add the potato, ginger, ground cumin and coriander and stir well. Continue cooking gently over a low heat for a few minutes, stirring until the potato is well coated with spices.

pour in the vegetable stock and bring to the boil. Reduce the heat, cover the pan and simmer gently for 15 minutes. Add the peas and chilli, and season to taste with salt and pepper. Continue cooking for 5 minutes over a low heat.

blend the soup in a food processor or blender until smooth and return to the pan. Place over a low heat and stir in the cream. Serve hot, garnished with coriander leaves.

Serves 4
Preparation time: *15 minutes*
Cooking time: *35–40 minutes*

clipboard: Ghee is used as a cooking fat in Indian cookery. It is clarified butter, the best being made from buffaloes' milk, which is twice as rich in fat as cows' milk. Clarified butter, which has had all the milk solids removed, can be heated to a high temperature without burning.

Minced Meat Samosas

2 tablespoons milk
oil for deep-frying
chutney, to serve

Dough
500 g/1 lb plain flour
1 teaspoon salt
175 g/6 oz soft margarine
150 ml/¼ pint water

Filling
1 tablespoon butter
1 small onion, chopped
½ teaspoon cumin seeds
250 g/8 oz minced beef
1 fresh green chilli, finely chopped
1 teaspoon salt
125 g/4 oz cooked peas
1 teaspoon chopped fresh coriander leaves
freshly ground black pepper

Serves 6
Preparation time: *1 hour*
Cooking time: *15–20 minutes*

sift the flour and salt into a large mixing bowl to make the samosa dough. Cut the margarine into small pieces and rub it into the flour with your fingertips, until the mixture resembles fine breadcrumbs. Stir in the water, a little at a time, until it is all amalgamated. Knead thoroughly until you have a smooth dough. Cover with a damp cloth

make the filling by melting the butter in a saucepan. Fry the onion and cumin seeds over a moderate heat, stirring occasionally for 5–7 minutes. Add the minced beef, chilli and salt and mix thoroughly. Reduce the heat and simmer for 10 minutes.

stir in the peas and continue cooking over a moderate heat for 5 minutes, or until the liquid has evaporated. Remove the pan from the heat and mix in the coriander and a pinch of pepper. Leave to cool before using to stuff the samosas.

divide the samosa dough into 12 equal portions and roll out each one to a thin circle, 18 cm/7 inch diameter. Cut each circle in half with a sharp knife and then cover the semi-circles with a damp cloth while you fill them one at a time.

brush the edges of each semi-circle with a little milk and spoon some filling on to the centre. Fold in the corners, overlapping them to form a cone. Fold over and seal the top to make a triangle. Deep-fry in hot oil in batches, until crisp and golden. Drain on absorbent kitchen paper and serve hot with chutney.

Vegetable Samosas

These crisp and spicy vegetable pasties are absolutely delicious served as a starter, accompanied by your favourite chutney.

1 quantity basic samosa dough (see Minced Meat Samosas, page 24)
2 tablespoons milk
oil for deep-frying
chutney, to serve

Filling
1 tablespoon ghee, or vegetable oil
pinch of asafoetida powder
2 teaspoons mustard seeds
500 g/1 lb potatoes, parboiled and diced
125 g/4 oz cooked peas
2 fresh green chillies, deseeded and chopped
1 teaspoon salt
1 teaspoon pomegranate seeds (optional)
1 teaspoon garam masala
2 tablespoons chopped fresh coriander leaves

make the filling: heat the ghee or oil in a frying pan and add the asafoetida powder, mustard seeds, potatoes, peas, chillies, salt and pomegranate seeds, if using. Stir well over a moderate heat for 2 minutes. Cover the pan, reduce the heat and cook gently for 10 minutes.

remove the pan from the heat and add the garam masala and chopped coriander. Stir well and then leave the filling to cool before using to stuff the samosas.

roll out the samosa dough and prepare the semi-circles as described previously (see Minced Meat Samosas, page 24). Use the vegetable filling to stuff the samosas and fold over, sealing the edges with milk. Remember to cover them with a damp cloth while you are assembling them.

heat the oil for deep-frying and then fry the samosas, a few at a time, until crisp and golden. Remove with a slotted spoon and drain on absorbent kitchen paper. Serve them hot with chutney.

Serves 6
Preparation time: *1 hour*
  (including making dough)
Cooking time: *10 minutes*

Spiced Fried Prawns

Marinated in tamarind water with a little turmeric, ginger, shallots, garlic and light soy sauce, these are an Eastern variation on prawn fritters.

500 g/1 lb cooked prawns
2 tablespoons tamarind water, or lemon juice
pinch of turmeric
1 teaspoon grated fresh root ginger
2 shallots or ½ onion, sliced
2 garlic cloves, crushed
1 tablespoon light soy sauce
150 ml/¼ pint oil for frying

Batter
75 g/3 oz rice flour or plain flour
4 tablespoons water
1 small egg beaten
salt and freshly ground black pepper

remove the heads and shells from the prawns, leaving the tails intact. Carefully remove the black vein that runs along the back of each prawn.

place the prawns in a bowl with the tamarind water, turmeric, ginger, shallots or onion, garlic and soy sauce. Stir well and set aside to marinate in a cool place for 30 minutes.

make the batter while the prawns are marinating. Put the flour in a bowl and gradually add the water. Season with a little salt and pepper and then beat in the egg. Beat lightly until the batter is smooth and free from lumps.

drain the marinade from the prawns and shallots and then dip them into the batter. Heat the oil in a frying pan or wok and fry the prawns and shallots in batches until crisp and golden on both sides. Remove and drain on absorbent kitchen paper. Serve hot with plain boiled rice or some hot sauce or chutney.

Serves 4
Preparation time: *15 minutes*, plus
30 minutes marinating time
Cooking time: *10 minutes*

Ekuri

You thought you knew everything there was to know about scrambled eggs, but that was before you tried this delicious Indian version, lightly spiced with fresh green chillies.

50 g/2 oz butter
1 onion, finely chopped
2 fresh green chillies, finely chopped
8 eggs, lightly beaten with 2 tablespoons water
1 tablespoon finely chopped fresh coriander leaves
salt

heat the butter in a pan, add the onion and fry until deep golden. Add the chillies and fry for 30 seconds, then add the eggs, coriander and salt to taste and cook, stirring until the eggs are scrambled and set. Serve hot.

Serves 4
Preparation time: *5 minutes*
Cooking time: *10 minutes*

clipboard: Chillies first grew in the Amazon region of South America and in Mexico, and it was some time before they reached India. The arrival of the chilli changed the flavour of Indian cooking. Until then, the only source of 'heat' had been the peppercorn and the mustard seed. Fresh chillies are easily available, either green, yellow or red, from supermarkets and grocers. The inner membrane and the seeds are the hottest part, so it is advisable to wear rubber gloves when you remove them. Slit the chilli lengthways down the centre, hold it under a cold tap and rub off the membrane and seeds. Whenever you handle chillies, be careful not to put your fingers anywhere near your eyes, as the pungent juices will irritate and sting them.

Pakora

Pakora are onion rings, spinach leaves and parboiled potatoes, which are dipped into a spicy batter and deep-fried until crisp and golden. Absolutely delicious!

125 g/4 oz gram (besan) flour
1 teaspoon salt
½ teaspoon chilli powder
about 150 ml/¼ pint water
2 fresh green chillies, finely chopped
1 tablespoon finely chopped fresh coriander leaves
1 teaspoon melted ghee or vegetable oil
for deep-frying
2 onions, sliced into rings
8 small fresh spinach leaves, washed
2–3 potatoes, parboiled and sliced

sift the flour, salt and chilli powder into a bowl. Stir in sufficient water to make a thick batter and beat well until smooth. Leave to stand for 30 minutes.

stir the chillies and coriander into the batter, then add the melted ghee or vegetable oil. Drop in the onion rings to coat thickly with batter.

heat the oil in a deep pan, drop in the onion rings and deep-fry until crisp and golden. Remove from the pan with a slotted spoon, drain on kitchen paper and keep warm.

dip the spinach leaves into the batter and deep-fry in the same way adding more oil to the pan if necessary. Finally, repeat the process with the potato slices. Serve hot.

Serves 4
Preparation time: *10 minutes*, plus
  standing time
Cooking time: *35 minutes*

clipboard: Coriander has bright green, lacy leaves and white flowers, and an intense flavour and perfume. The leaves, roots and seeds are all used in cooking, and the leaves make a particularly attractive garnish. Gram flour (also known as besun or chana dhaal flour) is made from lentils and is useful for people who are allergic to gluten, a component of all wheat products.

Prawn Kebabs

Giant Pacific prawns are not cheap but they're succulent and tasty. To prepare this dish, they're marinated in lemon juice and spices, and then quickly grilled on skewers.

2 tablespoons oil
1 tablespoon lemon juice
2 garlic cloves, crushed
1 teaspoon paprika
½ teaspoon chilli powder
½ teaspoon salt
½ teaspoon turmeric
1 tablespoon finely chopped fresh coriander leaves
12 giant Pacific prawns, peeled

place all the ingredients in a shallow dish, stirring to coat the prawns thoroughly. Cover and chill for several hours, stirring occasionally.

thread the prawns on to skewers or place in the grill pan, and cook under a preheated moderate grill for 3–4 minutes on each side, or until cooked. Spoon over the pan juices when turning.

Serves 4
Preparation time: *5 minutes*, plus
2–3 hours chilling time
Cooking time: *6–8 minutes*

clipboard: Turmeric grows wild in the tropical countries of southern Asia and belongs to the same family as ginger. It is often used in marinades and gives an attractive yellow colouring, reminiscent of saffron. Because of its colour, turmeric is also used as a dye, most notably in the yellow robes of Buddhist monks.

Fish

Fish in Coconut Milk

2 cloves, ground
4 green cardamoms, ground
2 fresh green chillies, crushed
2 garlic cloves, crushed
1 cm/½ inch piece of fresh root ginger, peeled and chopped
1 tablespoon vindaloo masala powder
lemon juice to mix
500 g/1 lb white fish fillets (e.g. sole, plaice)
2 tablespoons vegetable oil
1 onion, thinly sliced
300 ml/½ pint coconut milk
salt
1 tablespoon chopped fresh coriander leaves, to garnish

mix together the cloves, cardamoms, chillies, garlic, ginger, vindaloo masala powder and a little salt in a bowl. Stir in enough lemon juice to make a smooth, thick paste.

rinse the fish fillets and pat them dry with absorbent kitchen paper. Spread the prepared spicy paste thickly and evenly over the fish.

heat the oil in a large saucepan or deep frying pan, and fry the onion until soft and golden. Add the prepared fish fillets and fry on both sides until golden brown.

pour in the coconut milk and season to taste with salt. Cover the pan and cook gently over a low heat for 15 minutes. Serve the fish sprinkled with coriander.

Serves 4
Preparation time: *20 minutes*
Cooking time: *30 minutes*

clipboard: Coconut milk is essential in Indian cookery (see page 16). It can be made using either desiccated or fresh coconut, which gives a richer, more mellow flavour and a creamier consistency. But there is no need nowadays to extract coconut milk from the coconut. Canned coconut milk is widely available in supermarkets and specialist Indian food stores. It is unsweetened and works extremely well.

Curried Fish Balls

750 g/1½ lb white fish fillets (e.g. haddock or cod)
2 tablespoons lemon juice
1 egg
1½ teaspoons salt
50 g/2 oz chickpea, or gram (besan) flour
4 fresh green chillies, deseeded and chopped
1 onion, finely chopped
2 tablespoons breadcrumbs
vegetable oil for shallow-frying
freshly ground black pepper

Sauce

125 g/4 oz ghee, or 2½ tablespoons vegetable oil
1 large onion, thinly sliced
2 garlic cloves, thinly sliced
1 cinnamon stick
2 bay leaves
2 teaspoons ground cumin
2 teaspoons ground coriander
1½ teaspoons turmeric
1 teaspoon chilli powder
150 g/5 oz tomato purée
600 ml/1 pint Fish Stock (see page 11)
2 tablespoons lemon juice
50 g/2 oz desiccated coconut
seeds of 10 cardamoms, ground
2 teaspoons fenugreek seeds, ground
salt and freshly ground black pepper

arrange the fish fillets in an ovenproof dish and sprinkle with lemon juice. Cover with foil and stand in a roasting pan half-filled with water. Poach in a preheated oven at 160°C/325°F/Gas Mark 3 for 15 minutes. Remove and, when cool, flake the fish.

whisk the egg with the salt and a little pepper. Sift in the chickpea flour, whisking all the time until the batter is smooth.

add the flaked fish, chillies, onion and breadcrumbs to the batter. Stir well to make a stiff paste. Break off lumps and form into about 20 small balls. Heat the oil in a frying pan and shallow-fry the balls in batches until evenly browned. Drain and keep warm.

make the sauce: heat the ghee or oil and fry the onion and garlic for 5 minutes, until soft. Add all the spices and cook for 2 minutes. Add the tomato purée and bring to the boil. Add the remaining ingredients and cook over a medium heat for 10 minutes. Add the fish balls, simmer for 5 minutes and serve hot with rice.

Serves 4
Preparation time: *30 minutes*
Cooking time: *40 minutes*
Oven temperature: 160°C/325°F/Gas
   Mark 3

clipboard: Chickpeas are a rich source of carbohydrates, proteins, phosphorus, calcium and iron, and therefore deserve a place in any healthy diet. In India, they are ground into flour, which is also known as gram flour or besan. Chickpea flour is available in larger supermarkets and specialist Indian stores.

Charcoal-Grilled Fish

1–1.5 kg/2–3½ lb halibut, cleaned and washed
4 tablespoons lemon juice
2 teaspoons salt
1½ teaspoons freshly ground black pepper

Masala
1 large onion, peeled
1 garlic clove, peeled
1 tablespoon chopped fresh coriander leaves
4 teaspoons natural yogurt
2 teaspoons garam masala
1 teaspoon chilli powder
1 teaspoon ground coriander
1 teaspoon ground cumin
1 teaspoon ground fenugreek

line a large baking dish with a sheet of foil 2½ times the size of the fish. Make 4 or 5 deep cuts in each side of the fish. Rub the fish with lemon juice and sprinkle with salt and pepper. Place the fish on the foil and set this aside.

make the masala: put the onion and garlic in a food processor and chop them finely. Alternatively, chop them very finely with a knife or grate them on a grater.

place the onion and garlic in a bowl with the coriander, yogurt, garam masala, chilli powder, ground coriander, cumin and the fenugreek, and mix well.

smear this mixture over the fish and inside the cuts and the cavity. Draw up the sides of the foil to make a tent shape and seal the edges. Leave in a cool place to marinate for 4 hours.

bake in a preheated oven at 160°C/325°F/Gas Mark 3 for 20 minutes. Remove the fish carefully and finish cooking on a barbecue or on a wire rack in the oven.

Serves 4
Preparation time: *15 minutes*, plus
  4 hours marinating time
Cooking time: *25–30 minutes*
Oven temperature:
  160°C/325°F/Gas Mark 3

Fish Tandoori

A delicately flavoured yogurt tandoori marinade goes particularly well with fish. It is possible to buy ready-prepared tandoori marinades, but this home-made version is a winner.

4 halibut steaks, about 175 g/6 oz each
50 g/2 oz natural yogurt
2 tablespoons oil
2 tablespoons paprika
1 tablespoon ground cumin
1 teaspoon ground fennel seeds
1 teaspoon chilli powder
salt

To garnish
1 small lettuce, shredded
1 fennel bulb, sliced
lemon wedges

wash the halibut steaks under running cold water and then gently pat them dry with absorbent kitchen paper. Set aside while you prepare the tandoori mixture.

put the yogurt in a bowl with the oil, paprika, cumin, fennel seeds, chilli powder and a little salt. Mix well together.

place the halibut steaks in the bowl and rub well with the tandoori mixture. Cover the bowl and leave in a cool place to marinate for 4–5 hours.

transfer the marinated fish to a shallow, ovenproof baking dish. Bake uncovered in a preheated oven at 180°C/350°F/Gas Mark 4 for 20–25 minutes. Arrange the lettuce on a warm serving dish and place the fish on top. Spoon over the juices and serve garnished with lettuce, fennel and lemon wedges.

Serves 4
Preparation time: *15 minutes*, plus
  4–5 hours marinating time
Cooking time: *20–25 minutes*
Oven temperature:
  180°C/350°F/Gas Mark 4

Fish Kebabs

Fish kebabs need to be made with a fairly firm white fish, such as haddock, halibut or monkfish, or they will disintegrate too easily and will fall off the skewers.

5 cm/2 inch piece of fresh root ginger, crushed
1 garlic clove, crushed
2 teaspoons ground cumin
1 teaspoon freshly ground black pepper
1 teaspoon ground coriander
1 teaspoon garam masala
½ teaspoon ground cloves
1 teaspoon ground aniseed
75 ml/3 fl oz natural yogurt
1 kg/2 lb white fish fillets, skinned and cubed
4 small onions, peeled
oil for basting

To serve
lime wedges
Raita (see page 208)
fresh mint leaves

put the ginger, garlic, cumin, black pepper, coriander, garam masala, cloves and aniseed in a large bowl. Stir in the yogurt and mix together until well blended.

add the pieces of fish to the yogurt mixture and turn in the marinade. Leave in a cool place for at least 1 hour.

cut the onions into thick slices. Thread them on to some wooden kebab skewers, alternating with the marinated fish.

brush the kebabs with any remaining yogurt marinade and a little oil. Arrange on a grill pan and place under a preheated hot grill until cooked and lightly browned all over. Turn the kebabs occasionally and baste with oil and marinade as necessary. Serve with lime wedges and yogurt raita, scattered with fresh mint.

Serves 4
Preparation time: *15 minutes*, plus
1 hour marinating time
Cooking time: *10-15 minutes*

clipboard: Aniseed, also known as anise, has a strong liquorice-like flavour, which is loved by some but hated by others. It is often used in India in marinades and curries, particularly with fish.

Prawn Curry
with onion and garlic

50 g/2 oz ghee, or 1 tablespoon vegetable oil

1 small onion, sliced

2 garlic cloves, sliced

2 teaspoons ground coriander

½ teaspoon ground ginger

1 teaspoon turmeric

½ teaspoon ground cumin

½ teaspoon chilli powder

2 tablespoons vinegar

500 g/1 lb peeled prawns

200 ml/7 fl oz water

chopped fresh coriander leaves, to garnish

heat the ghee or oil in a large heavy-bottomed saucepan. Add the onion and garlic and fry gently over a low heat for 4–5 minutes, until golden and soft.

mix together the ground coriander, ginger, turmeric, cumin and chilli powder in a small bowl. Mix in the vinegar to make a smooth paste.

add the spicy paste to the onion and garlic mixture in the pan, and then fry gently for a further 3 minutes, stirring constantly with a wooden spoon.

tip in the prawns and turn gently with a wooden spoon until they are well coated with the spices. Stir in the water and then simmer over a gentle heat for 2–3 minutes. Serve immediately, garnished with coriander leaves, with plain boiled rice.

Serves 4
Preparation time: *15 minutes*
Cooking time: *12–15 minutes*

clipboard: Cumin is one of the most subtle and delicate of all the Indian spices. It blends remarkably well with coriander and other spices such as ginger and turmeric, as in this recipe. It goes particularly well with prawns and fish.

Barbecued King Prawns

I kg/2 lb king prawns
8 tablespoons lemon juice
1½ teaspoons salt
1½ teaspoons freshly ground black pepper
I teaspoon aniseed

Marinade
2 teaspoons coriander seeds
2 teaspoons fenugreek seeds
seeds of 20 cardamoms
1½ teaspoons black onion seeds (kalongi)
4 bay leaves
I large onion, chopped
3 garlic cloves, chopped
7 cm/3 inch piece of fresh root ginger, peeled and chopped
350 ml/12 fl oz natural yogurt
1½ teaspoons turmeric
125 g/4 oz melted ghee or vegetable oil
few drops of red food colouring

wash the prawns and remove the heads. Make a slit along the underside of each shell with a sharp knife and then slightly flatten each prawn. Place in a bowl and sprinkle with the lemon juice, salt and pepper. Mix well and then set aside.

make the marinade: spread the coriander, fenugreek, cardamom and black onion seeds on a baking tray. Add the bay leaves and place in a preheated oven at 200°C/400°F/Gas Mark 6 for 10–15 minutes. Remove and cool, then grind with a mortar and pestle.

place the onion, garlic and ginger in a blender or food processor with the yogurt and turmeric, and blend until smooth. Add the ground roasted spices and melted ghee or vegetable oil and blend again for 30 seconds. Add the food colouring.

pour the marinade over the prawns, cover and marinate in the refrigerator for 6–8 hours or overnight. Remove the prawns and thread on to skewers. Sprinkle with aniseed and barbecue (or grill) gently for about 5 minutes, turning frequently and brushing with the marinade. Serve hot.

Serves 4
Preparation time: *30 minutes*, plus
 6–8 hours marinating time
Cooking time: *5–10 minutes*
Oven temperature:
 200°C/400°F/Gas Mark 6

Spicy Steamed Mussels
with coconut and yogurt

1 kg/2 lb fresh mussels
125 g/4 oz ghee or 2½ tablespoons vegetable oil
1 large onion, finely chopped
2 garlic cloves, finely chopped
2 teaspoons desiccated coconut
2 teaspoons salt
1 teaspoon turmeric
1 teaspoon chilli powder
1 teaspoon freshly ground black pepper
150 ml/¼ pint vinegar
500 ml/17 fl oz natural yogurt
2 teaspoons garam masala
8 tablespoons lemon juice
fresh coriander leaves, to garnish

scrub the mussels under cold running water and remove the beards. Place in a large bowl, cover with fresh cold water and leave to soak for 20–30 minutes.

heat the ghee or oil in a large saucepan while the mussels are soaking; add the onion and garlic and fry gently for 5 minutes, or until soft. Add the coconut and salt and continue frying until the coconut begins to brown. Stir in the turmeric, chilli powder and pepper and fry for 1 further minute.

drain the mussels and discard any that are open. Add the vinegar and mussels to the pan, cover and turn up the heat. Cook over a high heat for 5 minutes, shaking the pan occasionally, until the mussels open. Remove from the heat. Discard any mussels that have not opened.

remove the empty half shells from the mussels and discard. Arrange the mussels in layers in a warm serving dish. Pour the cooking liquid into a blender or food processor, add the yogurt and garam masala and blend for 1 minute. Return to the pan and heat through without boiling. Pour over the mussels and serve, sprinkled with lemon juice and coriander.

Serves 4
Preparation time: *20 minutes*, plus
20–30 minutes soaking time
Cooking time: *10–12 minutes*

Baked Spiced Fish

Cod steaks are cooked in an interesting spice mixture, consisting of ginger, cloves, chillies, chilli powder, coriander leaves and lemon juice, to make a delicious combination of flavours.

4 tablespoons oil

125 g/4 oz grated fresh coconut

5 cm/2 inch piece of fresh root ginger, chopped

1 large onion, chopped

4 garlic cloves, finely chopped

2 fresh green chillies, deseeded and chopped

1 teaspoon chilli powder

2 tablespoons finely chopped fresh coriander leaves

4 tablespoons lemon juice

1 kg/2 lb cod steaks

salt

heat the oil in a pan, add the coconut, ginger, onion, garlic, chillies and chilli powder and fry gently until the onion is translucent. Add the coriander, lemon juice and salt to taste and simmer for 15 minutes or until the coconut is soft.

oil the bottom of a baking dish just large enough to hold the fish. Arrange the fish steaks side by side and pour over the spice mixture.

bake in a preheated moderate oven, 160°C/325°F/Gas Mark 3, for 25 minutes or until tender.

Serves 4
Preparation time: *35 minutes*
Cooking time: *40 minutes*
Oven temperature: 160°C/325°F/Gas
  Mark 3

clipboard: Along with the West Indies and west Africa, India is one of the largest growers of ginger for export. It is a must in many Indian dishes and is also used in baths for toning the system and for relieving muscular aches and pains.

Amotik

Tamarind is used in this mildly spiced fish dish to add a distinctive bittersweet flavour. Be particularly careful not to overcook the fish or it will disintegrate.

50 g/2 oz tamarind, soaked in 6 tablespoons
hot water for 30 minutes
4 tablespoons oil
750 g/1½ lb monkfish or other firm white fish, cubed
flour for dusting
I onion, chopped
4 fresh green chillies, finely chopped
2 garlic cloves, crushed
I teaspoon ground cumin seeds
½–I teaspoon chilli powder
I tablespoon vinegar
salt

strain the tamarind, squeezing out as much water as possible. Discard the tamarind and reserve the water.

heat the oil in a large pan. Lightly dust the fish with flour, add to the pan and fry quickly on both sides. Remove from the pan with a slotted spoon and set aside.

add the onion to the pan and fry until soft and golden. Add the tamarind water, chillies, garlic, cumin, chilli powder and salt to taste and cook for 10 minutes. Add the fish and any juices and the vinegar.

simmer, uncovered, for about 5 minutes.

Serves 4
Preparation time: *20 minutes*
Cooking time: about *20 minutes*

clipboard: The tamarind is a tall, evergreen tree which has been cultivated in India for centuries. Yellow flowers are followed by light brown, hairy pods, containing some 4–10 seeds surrounded by a sticky dark red paste. Tamarind can be bought either fresh, in rectangular blocks of compressed pulp and seeds, or as a thick concentrate which is less easily available in the shops. The compressed form, which is used in this recipe, has to be soaked for between 30 minutes and 1 hour.

Prawn Pilau

Basmati rice is a special variety of Indian rice, with small but long grains and a distinctive flavour. It is much prized by the Indians and is the best rice to use for this pilau.

375 g/12 oz Basmati rice
6 tablespoons ghee or vegetable oil
1 tablespoon coriander seeds, crushed
½ teaspoon turmeric
1 small pineapple, cubed or 1 x 250 g/8 oz can pineapple cubes, drained
250 g/8 oz frozen prawns, thawed
1 teaspoon salt
about 600 ml/1 pint Fish or Chicken Stock (see page 11)

To garnish
2 tablespoons ghee or vegetable oil
2 tablespoons sultanas
2 tablespoons cashew nuts
2 hard-boiled eggs, quartered
2 tablespoons chopped fresh coriander leaves

wash the rice under cold running water, then soak in running cold water for 30 minutes; drain thoroughly,

heat the ghee or vegetable oil in a large saucepan, add the coriander seeds and fry for 30 seconds. Add the turmeric and stir for a few seconds, then add the pineapple and fry, stirring for 30 seconds. Add the prawns, rice and salt. (If using a stock cube, omit the salt.) Fry, stirring, for 1 minute, then pour in enough stock to cover the rice by 5 mm/¼ inch. Bring to the boil, cover tightly and cook very gently for 25 minutes or until the rice is cooked and the liquid absorbed.

prepare the garnish while the rice is cooking: heat the ghee or vegetable oil in a small pan, add the sultanas and cashews and fry for 1–2 minutes until the sultanas are plump and the nuts lightly coloured.

transfer the rice to a warmed serving dish and gently fork in the sultanas and nuts. Arrange the egg quarters around the edge and sprinkle the coriander on top.

Serves 6
Preparation time: *10 minutes*, plus
30 minutes soaking time
Cooking time: *about 45 minutes*

Fish Fritters

These lightly spiced cod fritters are just the thing to tickle the taste buds. Neither too hot nor too bland, they're sure to satisfy even the fussiest of eaters.

6 tablespoons oil
2 onions, chopped
1 tablespoon ground coriander seeds
3 fresh green chillies, deseeded and chopped
1 teaspoon salt
1 teaspoon freshly ground black pepper
750 g/1½ lb cod fillets, skinned and cut into small pieces
2 tablespoons finely chopped fresh coriander leaves

Batter
125 g/4 oz chickpea or gram flour (besan)
½ teaspoon chilli powder
½ teaspoon salt
1 egg, beaten
7 tablespoons water

heat 3 tablespoons of the oil in a pan, add the onion and fry until just soft. Stir in the ground coriander, chillies, salt and pepper, then add the fish. Fry for 2 minutes, then cover and cook on a very low heat for 2 minutes. Break up the mixture with a fork and add the chopped coriander. Remove from the heat and set aside while making the batter.

sift the flour, chilli powder and salt into a bowl. Add the egg and water and beat well to make a smooth batter. Leave to stand for 30 minutes, then stir in the fish mixture.

heat the remaining oil in a frying pan and drop in small spoonfuls of the batter mixture. Fry on both sides until golden. Drain thoroughly and keep warm while frying the remainder.

Serves 4
Preparation time: *20 minutes*, plus 30 minutes standing time
Cooking time: about *20 minutes*

clipboard: Gram flour is ground chickpea flour. It is excellent for making batter and is often used in India instead of wheat flour.

Chicken

Chicken Biriyani

8 chicken drumsticks
175 g/6 oz ghee or 5 tablespoons vegetable oil
25 g/1 oz almonds, chopped
25 g/1 oz cashew nuts, chopped
1 large onion, finely chopped
4 bay leaves
425 g/14 oz long-grain rice
900 ml/1½ pints warm water
½ teaspoon saffron strands (optional)
2 tablespoons melted butter
salt
1 small red chilli, finely sliced, to garnish
coriander leaves, to garnish

Paste

1 teaspoon garam masala
1 small onion, chopped
2 garlic cloves, crushed
5 cm/2 inch piece of fresh root ginger
150 ml/¼ pint natural yogurt
1 teaspoon salt

Biriyani spices

4 cloves
8 black peppercorns
4 green cardamoms
1 black cardamom, crushed
5 cm/2 inch piece of cinnamon stick
½ teaspoon turmeric

grind all the paste ingredients together in a mortar or food processor to make a smooth mixture. Rub this paste over the chicken drumsticks and leave them to marinate for 30 minutes.

heat the ghee or oil in a frying pan and fry the almonds and cashews until golden brown. Remove with a slotted spoon and drain on absorbent kitchen paper. Set aside for the garnish. Add the onion to the pan and fry until golden. Remove half of the onion and keep for the garnish.

mix together the biriyani spices without grinding. Add them with the bay leaves to the onion in the pan, stir well and then add the chicken. Cook over a moderate heat for 20 minutes. Stir in the rice and then add the warm water and some salt. Cover and cook for 15–20 minutes until the rice is tender and all the water absorbed.

steep the saffron in a little water for 5 minutes, if using. Add the melted butter and stir into the rice. Serve garnished with the reserved fried onions and nuts, chilli slices and coriander leaves.

Serves 4
Preparation time: *30 minutes*, plus
30 minutes marinating time
Cooking time: *50 minutes*

clipboard: Saffron is made from the dried stamens of a species of crocus. Over 4,000 blooms are required to yield 25 g (1 oz) of saffron, which is why it is the most expensive and highly prized of all the spices. It is available either as whole threads or ground into a powder. It is better to buy threads than powder, as the latter is easily adulterated, especially in the Far East where marigold or safflower stamens are often substituted for the real thing.

Chicken Korma

This mild curry, in which yogurt makes a delicately creamy sauce, is a favourite with many people who do not care for anything too hot or spicy.

175 ml/6 fl oz natural yogurt
2 teaspoons turmeric
3 garlic cloves, sliced
1 x 1.5 kg/3 lb roasting chicken, skinned and cut into 8 pieces
125 g/4 oz ghee or 4 tablespoons vegetable oil
1 large onion, sliced
1 teaspoon ground ginger
5 cm/2 inch piece of cinnamon stick
5 cloves
5 cardamom pods
1 tablespoon crushed coriander seeds
1 teaspoon ground cumin
½ teaspoon chilli powder
1 teaspoon salt
1½ tablespoons desiccated coconut
2 teaspoons toasted almonds, to garnish
coriander leaves, to garnish

put the yogurt, turmeric and one of the garlic cloves in a blender or food processor and blend to a smooth purée.

place the chicken pieces in a shallow dish and pour the yogurt mixture over them. Cover the dish and leave to marinate in the refrigerator overnight.

heat the ghee or oil in a large, heavy-bottomed saucepan and add the onion and remaining garlic. Fry gently for 4–5 minutes until soft. Add the spices and salt and fry for a further 3 minutes, stirring constantly.

add the chicken pieces with the yogurt marinade and coconut and mix well. Cover the pan with a tightly fitting lid and then simmer gently for 45 minutes, or until the chicken is cooked and tender. Transfer to a warmed serving dish and scatter with the almonds and coriander leaves.

Serves 4
Preparation time: *15 minutes*, plus overnight marinating time
Cooking time: *55 minutes*

Tandoori Chicken

8 chicken quarters
8 tablespoons lemon juice
2 teaspoons salt

Marinade
10 cloves
2 teaspoons coriander seeds
2 teaspoons cumin seeds
seeds of 10 cardamoms
2 onions, chopped
4 garlic cloves, chopped
7 cm/3 inch piece of fresh root ginger, peeled and chopped
2 teaspoons chilli powder
2 teaspoons freshly ground black pepper
1½ teaspoons turmeric
350 ml/12 fl oz natural yogurt
few drops of red food colouring (optional)

remove the skin from the chicken pieces and discard. Wash and dry the chicken and then score each piece several times with a sharp knife. Place in a large dish and sprinkle with the lemon juice and salt. Rub this mixture in well, then cover and leave in a cool place for 1 hour.

prepare the marinade while the chicken is standing: spread the cloves, coriander, cumin and cardamom seeds on a baking tray and roast in a preheated oven at 200°C/400°F/Gas Mark 6 for 10–15 minutes. Remove and, when cool, grind them coarsely in a mortar.

put the onions, garlic and ginger in a blender or food processor and sprinkle with the chilli powder, black pepper and turmeric. Add the yogurt and ground roasted spices and strain in the lemon juice from the chicken. Blend until smooth, adding some red food colouring if wished.

place the chicken pieces in a single layer in a large roasting pan and pour over the marinade. Cover the pan and leave in the refrigerator to marinate for at least 24 hours, turning occasionally. Cook in a preheated oven at 200°C/400°F/Gas Mark 6 for 20 minutes and then place under a hot grill until crisp. Serve hot or cold.

Serves 8
Preparation time: *45 minutes*, plus
  1 hour standing time, plus
  24 hours marinating time
Cooking time: *30 minutes*
Oven temperature: 200°C/400°F/
  Gas Mark 6

Chicken Vindaloo

A chicken vindaloo is a fiery curry, and strictly not for the fainthearted! If you're worried about it being too hot, reduce the quantity of vindaloo masala.

2 tablespoons vindaloo masala
2 teaspoons vinegar
3 teaspoons salt
1 x 1.5 kg/3 lb chicken, cut into pieces
6 tablespoons mustard or vegetable oil
4 bay leaves
1 teaspoon green cardamom seeds
1 large onion, thinly sliced
2 teaspoons turmeric
1 teaspoon cayenne
10 garlic cloves, crushed
15 g/½ oz fresh root ginger, thinly sliced
2 tomatoes, skinned and quartered
150 ml/¼ pint tamarind or lemon juice
2 teaspoons desiccated coconut

put the vindaloo masala, vinegar and 2 teaspoons of the salt in a bowl and then mix well to make a smooth paste.

wash and dry the chicken pieces and then score each piece several times with a sharp knife. Rub the paste all over them and leave in a cool place to marinate for 1 hour.

heat the mustard oil in a large saucepan and stir in the bay leaves and cardamom seeds. Add the onion and fry until light brown. Stir in the turmeric and cayenne and add the chicken pieces. Cook, stirring occasionally, for 15 minutes. Add the reserved salt, garlic, ginger and tomatoes and cook for 10 minutes, stirring.

add the tamarind or lemon juice to the pan when the fat starts to separate. Stir well, cover and simmer gently for about 25 minutes or until the chicken is tender. Sprinkle with coconut and serve.

Serves 6
Preparation time: *15 minutes*, plus
1 hour marinating time
Cooking time: *55 minutes*

Chicken and Lentils

with spinach and tomatoes

500 g/1 lb dried split peas or lentils (e.g. moong dhal)

1.2 litres/2 pints water

175 g/6 oz ghee or 5 tablespoons vegetable oil

2 large onions, sliced

4 garlic cloves, sliced

6 cloves

6 cardamoms

1½ teaspoons ground ginger

2 teaspoons garam masala

2½ teaspoons salt

1 x 1.5 kg/3 lb roasting chicken, skinned, boned and cut into 8 pieces

500 g/1 lb frozen whole-leaf spinach

4 large tomatoes, skinned and chopped

wash the split peas or lentils and then place in a large saucepan. Add the measured water and bring to the boil. Cover the pan, lower the heat and simmer for 15 minutes.

heat the ghee or oil in a large, heavy-bottomed saucepan, add the onions and garlic and fry for 4–5 minutes until soft. Add the spices and salt and fry for 3 minutes, stirring constantly. Add the chicken and brown on all sides, then remove and drain on absorbent kitchen paper.

add the spinach and tomatoes to the saucepan and fry gently over a low heat for 10 minutes stirring occasionally.

mash the peas or lentils in their cooking water and then stir them into the spinach mixture. Return the chicken to the pan, cover with a tightly fitting lid and simmer gently for 45 minutes, or until the chicken is cooked and tender.

Serves 4
Preparation time: *30 minutes*
Cooking time: *1¼ hours*

Roast Chicken with Almonds

2 tablespoons oil
75 g/3 oz ghee or 1½ tablespoons sunflower oil
3 onions, chopped
pinch of ground saffron
300 ml/½ pint natural yogurt
1 tablespoon coriander seeds
1 teaspoon cumin seeds
8 cloves
6 cardamom pods
1 x 1.5 kg/3 lb roasting chicken
125 g/4 oz blanched slivered almonds
50 g/2 oz raisins
salt
freshly ground black pepper

heat the oil and two-thirds of the ghee or sunflower oil in a frying pan and add the onions. Fry until golden brown. Mix in the saffron and yogurt and set aside to cool.

put the coriander and cumin seeds, salt and pepper, cloves and cardamoms in a mortar, and pound well. Rub this spice mixture all over the chicken and place in a roasting pan.

put the chicken in a preheated oven at 190°C/375°F/Gas Mark 5 for about 1¼ hours until the chicken is cooked and tender. After about 20 minutes, baste the chicken with the yogurt mixture and return to the oven. Keep basting the chicken at regular intervals.

heat the reserved ghee or sunflower oil in a frying pan and, while the chicken is cooking, fry the almonds until they start to turn golden brown. Add the raisins and stir well. Remove from the heat. Serve the chicken, topped with the almonds and raisins, with some plain boiled rice.

Serves 4–6
Preparation time: *20 minutes*
Cooking time: *1¼ hours*
Oven temperature:
  190°C/375°F/Gas Mark 5

Chicken Pilau

375 g/12 oz Basmati rice
5 tablespoons ghee or vegetable oil
5 cm/2 inch piece of cinnamon stick
8 cloves
6 cardamom seeds
2 garlic cloves, crushed
1 teaspoon chilli powder
1 tablespoon fennel seeds
4 chicken portions, skinned
5 tablespoons natural yogurt
1 teaspoon ground saffron
1½ teaspoons salt
600 ml/1 pint Chicken Stock (see page 11)

To garnish
2 large onions, sliced
4 tablespoons ghee
fresh coriander leaves

wash the rice thoroughly and drain. Place in a large bowl and cover with fresh cold water. Leave to soak for 30 minutes and then drain well.

heat the ghee or oil in a large saucepan and add the cinnamon, cloves and cardamom seeds. Fry briskly for 30 seconds and then stir in the garlic, chilli powder and fennel seeds. Fry for a further 30 seconds.

add the chicken portions and fry, turning occasionally, for 5 minutes. Stir in the yogurt, a spoonful at a time, and then cover the pan and simmer for 25 minutes.

add the rice, saffron and salt. Fry, stirring until the rice is glistening and coated with spices. Add enough stock to cover the rice by 5 mm/¼ inch and bring to the boil. Reduce the heat to a bare simmer and cook, covered tightly, for 20 minutes or until the rice is cooked.

fry the onions in the ghee or oil in another pan. Use to garnish the pilau with the coriander leaves.

Serves 4
Preparation time: *20 minutes*, plus
 30 minutes soaking time
Cooking time: *1–1¼ hours*

clipboard: Wild fennel has large, long, light greenish-brown seeds which have a slight aniseed flavour. They are much used in Indian cookery with meat, fish and vegetables, and are also used in spice mixtures. Whole roasted fennel seeds are also chewed in India after a meal, when they are said to have a digestive effect.

Chicken Tikka

Pieces of chicken marinated in yogurt flavoured with ginger, cloves, chilli powder, coriander seeds and lemon juice make for a delicately spiced combination.

150 g/5 oz natural yogurt
1 tablespoon grated fresh root ginger
2 garlic cloves, crushed
1 teaspoon chilli powder
1 tablespoon ground coriander seeds
½ teaspoon salt
4 tablespoons lemon juice
2 tablespoons oil
750 g/1½ lb chicken breasts, skinned, boned and cubed

To garnish
1 onion, sliced
2 tomatoes, quartered
4 lemon twists

mix together in a bowl all the ingredients except the chicken. Drop the chicken cubes into the marinade. Cover and leave in the refrigerator overnight.

thread the chicken on to 4 skewers and cook under a preheated hot grill for 5–6 minutes, turning frequently.

remove the chicken from the skewers and arrange on individual serving plates. Garnish with onion, tomato and lemon to serve.

Serves 4
Preparation time: *15 minutes*, plus overnight marinating time
Cooking time: *5–6 minutes*

clipboard: The principal purpose of a marinade is to flavour food, but it also makes certain meats more tender by softening the fibres.

Chicken Tikka Masala

Chicken Tikka (see page 78), marinated and threaded on to skewers but not cooked
2 tablespoons chopped fresh coriander leaves
juice of ½ lime

Masala sauce
50 g/2 oz ghee or vegetable oil
2 onions, thinly sliced
2.5 cm/1 inch piece of fresh root ginger, finely chopped
2 garlic cloves, crushed
6 cardamoms, bruised
2 teaspoons garam masala
2 teaspoons ground coriander
1 teaspoon chilli powder, or to taste
300 ml/½ pint double cream
2 tablespoons tomato purée
4 tablespoons hot water
½ teaspoon sugar
½ teaspoon salt

To garnish
chopped coriander leaves
diced tomato

make the masala sauce by heating the ghee or vegetable oil in a large flameproof casserole; add the onions, ginger and garlic and fry over a gentle heat, stirring frequently, for about 5 minutes until softened but not coloured.

add the spices and fry, stirring, for 1–2 minutes until fragrant, then add the cream, tomato purée, water, sugar and salt. Bring slowly to the boil over a moderate heat, stirring, then lower the heat and simmer gently, stirring occasionally, for 10–15 minutes. Remove the pan from the heat and leave to stand while cooking the chicken.

barbecue or grill the Chicken Tikka according to the recipe instructions on page 78, and then remove the cubes of chicken from the skewers.

tip the chicken into the masala sauce, return to a low heat and simmer, stirring, for about 5 minutes. Add the chopped coriander leaves and lime juice, and taste for seasoning. Serve immediately, garnished with coriander leaves and diced tomato.

Serves 4
Preparation time: *20 minutes, plus marinating*
Cooking time: *40–45 minutes*

clipboard: The aroma of the cardamom is contained within the seeds – small black seeds within a papery pod. Cardamom is related to ginger and is widely grown in the tropical regions of India.

Kashmiri Chicken

The addition of natural yogurt towards the end of the cooking time gives this a deliciously mild and creamy flavour, which makes a wonderful contrast to all the spices.

50 g/2 oz ghee or vegetable oil
3 large onions, finely sliced
10 peppercorns
10 cardamoms
5 cm/2 inch piece of cinnamon stick
5 cm/2 inch piece of fresh root ginger, chopped
2 garlic cloves, finely chopped
1 teaspoon chilli powder
2 teaspoons paprika
1.5 kg/3 lb chicken pieces, skinned
250 ml/8 fl oz natural yogurt
salt

heat the ghee or vegetable oil in a deep, lidded frying pan. Add the onions, peppercorns, cardamoms and cinnamon and fry until the onions are golden. Add the ginger, garlic, chilli powder, paprika and salt to taste and fry for 2 minutes, stirring occasionally.

add the chicken pieces and fry until browned. Gradually add the yogurt, stirring constantly. Cover and cook gently for about 30 minutes.

Serves 6
Preparation time: *20 minutes*
Cooking time: *30–35 minutes*

clipboard: Paprika is made from mild varieties of capsicum, or sweet pepper, which have had their seeds and inner membranes removed before being dried and ground. It should be bought in small quantities and replaced often, as its flavour and colour both deteriorate rapidly. It should be a bright red colour, which shows that it is fresh.

Palak Murg

This mild chicken dish is both quick and simple to make, and the combination of chicken with ginger, coriander and chilli powder is a highly successful one.

3 tablespoons oil
2 onions, chopped
2 garlic cloves, crushed
2.5 cm/1 inch piece of fresh root ginger, chopped
2 teaspoons ground coriander seeds
1 teaspoon chilli powder
750 g/1½ lb chicken legs and thighs, skinned
750 g/1½ lb fresh spinach, washed and trimmed
milk (optional)
salt

heat the oil in a large saucepan, add the onions and fry until golden. Add the garlic, ginger, coriander, chilli powder and salt to taste and fry gently for 2 minutes, stirring.

add the chicken and fry on all sides until browned. Add the spinach, stir well, cover and simmer for 35 minutes until the chicken is tender.

stir in 2–3 tablespoons milk if the mixture becomes too dry during cooking. If there is too much liquid left at the end, uncover and cook for a few minutes until it has evaporated.

Serves 4
Preparation time: *20 minutes*
Cooking time: *35–40 minutes*

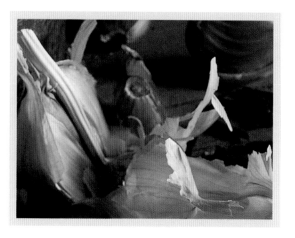

clipboard: Fresh ginger is often required in Indian cooking. It freezes very well – simply wrap it in cling film or in a small freezer bag. You can then use exactly the amount you need, and return the rest to the freezer for use later. Ginger can also be kept in the refrigerator in a tightly sealed jar of dry sherry. Ground ginger is not an acceptable substitute for the real thing.

Chicken Molee

with ginger and creamed coconut

about 3 tablespoons oil

4 chicken breasts, skinned, boned and cut into 3–4 pieces

6 cardamoms

6 cloves

5 cm/2 inch piece of cinnamon stick

I large onion, finely sliced

2 garlic cloves

3.5 cm/I½ inch piece of fresh root ginger, chopped

3 fresh green chillies, deseeded

4 tablespoons lemon juice

I teaspoon turmeric

50 g/2 oz creamed coconut

150 ml/¼ pint hot water

salt

heat the oil in a pan, add the chicken and fry quickly all over. Remove with a slotted spoon and set aside.

add a little more oil to the pan if necessary and fry the cardamoms, cloves and cinnamon for 1 minute. Add the onion and fry until soft.

place the garlic, ginger, chillies and lemon juice in a blender or food processor and work to a smooth paste. Add to the pan with the turmeric and cook for 5 minutes.

melt the coconut in the hot water and add to the pan with salt to taste. Simmer for 2 minutes, then add the chicken pieces and any juices. Simmer for 15–20 minutes until tender.

Serves 4
Preparation time: *25 minutes*
Cooking time: *25–30 minutes*

clipboard: Cinnamon is the thinly rolled inner bark of an evergreen tree that grows abundantly in southern India. It is often used in India to flavour meat and rice dishes, and is one of the ingredients in commercially manufactured curry powder.

Chicken Makhani

Tomatoes and butter are the characteristic ingredients of a makhani, a refined and elegant dish. Naan bread is a good accompaniment.

750 g/1½ lb skinned, boned chicken breasts or thighs, cut into 5 cm/2 inch pieces
3 tablespoons vegetable oil

Marinade
3 large fresh red chillies, deseeded and chopped
4 garlic cloves, crushed
2 teaspoons toasted cumin seeds, crushed
1 teaspoon garam masala
½ teaspoon salt
2 tablespoons fresh coriander leaves
4 tablespoons lemon juice
150 ml/¼ pint natural yogurt

Sauce
1.5 kg/3 lb ripe tomatoes, quartered
50 g/2 oz butter
150 ml/¼ pint double cream
salt

To garnish
1 tablespoon double cream
sprigs of fresh coriander

Serves 6
Preparation time: *15 minutes*, plus 3 hours marinating time
Cooking time: *2¼ hours*

start by making the marinade. Place the chillies, garlic and cumin seeds in a blender or food processor and blend briefly before adding the remaining ingredients and blending to produce a paste.

transfer the marinade to a non-metallic bowl. Add the chicken to the marinade, turning to coat them evenly. Cover and refrigerate for 3 hours.

prepare the sauce while the chicken is marinating. Place the tomatoes in a large saucepan and cook them gently, with no added water, for about 20 minutes or until they are tender. Then rub them through a fine sieve into a clean saucepan. Simmer the tomato pulp, stirring occasionally for about 50 minutes until it is thick and reduced.

stir in the butter and a little salt and cook the sauce over a medium heat, stirring often, for a further 30 minutes until it is thick. Stir in the cream and heat it through. Taste and adjust the amount of salt if necessary and set the sauce aside.

heat the oil in a large heavy-bottomed sauté pan. Remove the chicken pieces from their marinade, reserving the marinade and fry gently to seal them, for about 5 minutes. Add the marinade to the pan, increase the heat and cook, stirring frequently, for a further 12 minutes or until the chicken is cooked through.

reduce the heat and pour the tomato sauce over the chicken. Simmer gently for a further 5 minutes. Transfer the chicken to a serving dish and garnish with a swirl of cream and a few coriander sprigs.

Bangalore Chicken Curry

This 'green' curry from central southern India is made with a lot of fresh coriander and fresh green chillies

3 tablespoons ghee or vegetable oil

2 onions, thinly sliced

6 garlic cloves, chopped

1 teaspoon turmeric

1½ teaspoons ground dhana jeera (¾ teaspoon ground coriander and ¾ teaspoon ground cumin)

40 g/1½ oz fresh coriander leaves

3 large fresh green chillies, deseeded and chopped

1 x 1.75 kg/3½ lb chicken, cut into 8 pieces

150 ml/¼ pint Chicken Stock (see page 11)

300 ml/½ pint coconut milk

1 teaspoon salt

1 tablespoon lemon juice

fresh coriander leaves, to garnish

heat the ghee or oil in a large heavy-bottomed sauté pan. Add the onions and fry over a medium heat, stirring frequently, for about 5 minutes or until they are softened and golden.

stir in the garlic, turmeric and dhana jeera and cook, stirring, for a further 3 minutes.

place the coriander leaves and green chillies in a blender or food processor and blend to a paste. Add this paste to the pan, reduce the heat to very low and cook, stirring constantly, for a further 10 minutes.

add the chicken pieces to the pan, turn them in the spice mixture to coat them evenly, then add the stock, coconut milk and salt. Bring to the boil, then reduce the heat, cover and simmer, stirring and turning the chicken occasionally, for about 50 minutes or until the juices from the chicken run clear when tested with a skewer. Stir in the lemon juice and taste and adjust the amount of salt if necessary.

transfer the cooked chicken pieces to a serving dish and keep them warm. Increase the heat and boil the curry sauce for 5–8 minutes to thicken it. Pour it over the chicken and garnish with coriander.

Serves 6
Preparation time: *20 minutes*
Cooking time: *1 hour 20 minutes*

Balti Chicken
with green pepper

6 tablespoons vegetable oil
1 onion, chopped
½ teaspoon ground turmeric
1 teaspoon ground coriander
1 teaspoon ground cumin
1 teaspoon chilli powder
2 tablespoons water
750 g/1½ lb skinned, boned chicken, cubed
1 kg/2 lb tomatoes, chopped
1 large green pepper, deseeded and cut into squares
4–6 garlic cloves, chopped
2 fresh green chillies, chopped
salt

To garnish
2 tomatoes, quartered
sprigs of fresh coriander

heat the oil in a large wok or heavy-bottomed saucepan, add the onion and fry until soft. Mix the turmeric, coriander, cumin and chilli powder with the water. Stir this spice mixture into the onions and cook until the liquid has evaporated, about 3–4 minutes.

add the chicken and fry on all sides, then add the tomatoes and a pinch of salt to taste. Cover and cook for 15 minutes.

stir in the green pepper, garlic, and chillies. Cook, uncovered, until all the tomato juices have evaporated and the chicken is cooked through. Serve hot, garnished with the tomatoes and sprigs of coriander.

Serves 4–6
Preparation time: *20 minutes*
Cooking time: *30–40 minutes*

clipboard: Garlic should be stored in a cool place, either laid out flat or hanging in bunches to improve aeration. Generally speaking, white garlic lasts about 6 months, and pink garlic nearly a year.

Lamb and Pork

Lamb Kebabs

Minced lamb is made into a sausage with spices and lemon juice, and the 'sausages' are then threaded on to skewers and grilled.

750 g/1½ lb lean lamb, minced
1 teaspoon grated fresh root ginger
1 large onion, finely chopped
25 g/1 oz chickpea or gram flour (besan)
2 fresh green chillies, finely chopped
1 teaspoon green mango powder
1 tablespoon salt
2 tablespoons lemon juice
1 egg
2 tablespoons chopped fresh coriander leaves
50 g/2 oz melted ghee or 1 tablespoon vegetable oil
lime wedges, to garnish

Spices
½ teaspoon poppy seeds, roasted and ground
1 teaspoon garam masala
1 tablespoon yellow or red chilli powder
½ teaspoon freshly ground black pepper
1 teaspoon black cumin seeds, roasted and ground
1 tablespoon ground coriander seeds

mix the minced meat, ginger, onion, chickpea or gram flour, chillies, mango powder, salt and lemon juice together with all the spices. Set aside for 30 minutes to allow the flavours to develop.

work the egg and chopped coriander into the minced meat mixture. Continue kneading the mixture until it becomes sticky.

divide the minced meat mixture into 18 equal-sized portions and then form each piece between your hands into a sausage shape.

thread the 'sausages' on to skewers. For longer kebabs, flatten them out on the skewers. Cook under a preheated hot grill or over charcoal, turning frequently. Brush the kebabs with melted ghee or oil while they are cooking. Serve hot, garnished with lime wedges.

Serves 6
Preparation time: *30 minutes*, plus
30 minutes standing time
Cooking time: *20–30 minutes*

clipboard: Mango powder, also known as aamchoor, is a sour-tasting powder made from raw mangoes. It is sold in jars in specialist Indian food stores.

Lamb with Almonds

50 g/2 oz ghee or 1 tablespoon vegetable oil
125 g/4 oz onion, finely chopped
5 small green cardamoms
½ teaspoon ground turmeric
1 teaspoon chilli powder
1 teaspoon ground cumin
1½ teaspoons paprika
1 teaspoon ground coriander
150 ml/¼ pint natural yogurt
250 g/8 oz tomatoes, skinned and chopped
500 g/1 lb boned leg of lamb, cut into 2.5 cm/1 inch cubes
salt
chopped fresh coriander leaves, to garnish

Masala
15 g/½ oz fresh root ginger, peeled and chopped
6 garlic cloves, peeled
1 blade of mace
¼ teaspoon ground nutmeg
4 cloves
1 tablespoon dry roasted poppy seeds
12 peppercorns
50 g/2 oz blanched almonds
seeds of 2 large cardamoms

make the masala first: grind the ginger, garlic, mace, nutmeg, cloves, poppy seeds, peppercorns, almonds and cardamom seeds. Add a little water to make a fine paste.

heat the ghee or oil in a deep frying pan and gently fry the onion until light brown. Add the small green cardamoms and stir in the masala paste. Fry over a low heat for 2 minutes.

add the turmeric, chilli powder, cumin, paprika and coriander to the pan, and fry over a gentle heat for a further 1–2 minutes.

stir in the yogurt and tomatoes and then the lamb with a little salt. Cover and cook over a low heat for 40–50 minutes, sprinkling with a little water if necessary. Serve garnished with coriander.

Serves 4
Preparation time: *30 minutes*
Cooking time: *1¼ hours*

clipboard: Yogurt is often used in Indian cooking to add a sharp creaminess. Use a natural yogurt – preferably a thin tart-flavoured variety rather then the milder, creamier Greek type. If you use a 'set' yogurt, always stir it a little to break up the 'setting' before adding it to the dish.

Kheema do Pyaza

Minced lamb is delicately spiced and then simmered with natural yogurt and tomatoes until the meat is cooked — an unusual combination.

500 g/1 lb onions
4 tablespoons oil
2.5 cm/1 inch piece of fresh root ginger, chopped
1 garlic clove, finely chopped
2 fresh green chillies, finely chopped
1 teaspoon turmeric
1 teaspoon ground coriander seeds
1 teaspoon ground cumin seeds
750 g/1½ lb minced lamb
150 g/5 oz natural yogurt
1 × 250 g/8 oz can tomatoes
salt

chop 375 g/12 oz of the onions finely; thinly slice the remainder.

measure 2 tablespoons of the oil into a pan, add the chopped onion and fry until golden. Add the ginger, garlic, chillies and spices and fry for 2 minutes. Add the minced lamb and cook, stirring to break up, until well browned.

stir in the yogurt, spoon by spoon, until it is absorbed, then add the tomatoes with their juice and salt to taste. Bring to the boil, stir well, cover and simmer for 20 minutes or until the meat is cooked.

heat the remaining oil while the lamb is cooking and fry the sliced onions until brown and crisp. Transfer the meat mixture to a warmed serving dish and sprinkle with the fried onion.

Serves 4
Preparation time: *30 minutes*
Cooking time: *30–40 minutes*

Roghan Ghosht

This unusual combination of cubed lamb cooked gently in mildly spiced yogurt with chopped fresh mint leaves and flaked almonds is absolutely delicious.

4 tablespoons oil
2 onions, finely chopped
750 g/1½ lb boned leg of lamb, cubed
2 × 150 g/5 oz cartons natural yogurt
2 garlic cloves, peeled
2.5 cm/1 inch piece of fresh root ginger
2 fresh green chillies
1 tablespoon coriander seeds
1 teaspoon cumin seeds
1 teaspoon chopped fresh mint leaves
1 teaspoon chopped fresh coriander leaves
6 cardamoms
6 cloves
2.5 cm/1 inch piece of cinnamon stick
125 g/4 oz flaked almonds
salt

heat 2 tablespoons of the oil in a pan, add half of the onions and fry until golden. Add the lamb and 175 g/6 oz of the yogurt, stir well, cover and simmer for 20 minutes.

place the garlic, ginger, chillies, coriander seeds, cumin seeds, mint, fresh coriander and 2–3 tablespoons yogurt in a blender or food processor and work to a paste.

take a large saucepan and heat the remaining oil, add the cardamoms, cloves and cinnamon and fry for 1 minute, stirring. Add the remaining onion and the prepared paste and fry for 5 minutes, stirring constantly.

add the lamb and yogurt mixture, and salt to taste, stir well and bring to simmering point. Cover and cook for 30 minutes. Add the almonds and cook for a further 15 minutes, until the meat is tender.

Serves 4
Preparation time: *30 minutes*
Cooking time: *1 hour 15 minutes*

Utensils

Turning bowl

Ladle

Measuring jug

Turning bowl
A turning bowl is a useful piece of equipment. It is used for mixing, beating or folding mixtures. It has a built-in stand to support it and to stop it slipping while you work. It can be used for working at different angles. The stainless steel surface is not only hard wearing but also very easy to keep clean.

Measuring jug
A measuring jug is a standardized measure of liquid. It has a handle and a good pouring lip. It is usually marked with both metric and imperial measures. It is available in glass, plastic or stainless steel. It is advisable to check before purchasing a jug that it is dishwasher safe.

Whisk
A whisk is an essential beating tool, which is used to blend ingredients and to incorporate air into batter or cake mixtures. Whisks come in a variety of different shapes and sizes: small ones are used for sauces, while the larger balloon whisk is the most popular and commonly used. A whisk is useful, too, for rescuing a lumpy sauce.

Ladle
A ladle is used as a serving utensil. A deep, long-handled spoon, it is generally used to transfer a soup or stew from the pan to the serving dish. It is usually made of stainless steel, which is hard wearing and easy to keep clean.

Whisk

Frying pan

Skillet

Skimmer

Turner

Frying pan

The best frying pan is made of a heavy-gauge, heat-conducting metal, which allows heat to be transmitted rapidly and evenly. It should have a wide, flat base and shallow sides, sloping outwards to give space for lifting and turning food. A long handle means that it is easy to lift.

Turner

A turner, or fish slice, is an indispensable piece of kitchen equipment, which will come in handy daily. It is a wide-blade implement, which is used to lift, turn and transfer food – such as rashers of bacon, fried eggs, pieces of meat or fillets of fish – from the pan or baking sheet to the serving dish. It is usually made of stainless steel, as it is both hard wearing and easy to maintain, and will last you for many years.

Skimmer

A skimmer is a shallow, long-handled spoon, which is perforated all over in order that food may be removed from a pan and, in the process, any unwanted liquid will simply drain away. Skimmers are usually made of stainless steel.

Skillet

A skillet is a flat, wide pan, which is used for rapid cooking purposes on top of the cooker. It can be used either to fry food, or to make sauces. A skillet should be an efficient heat conductor and often has a non-stick finish.

Lamb Korma

Mild and creamy, lamb korma is made with cubed leg of lamb, lightly spiced with a subtle combination of spices and cooked in creamy natural yogurt.

5 tablespoons oil
6 cardamoms
6 cloves
6 peppercorns
2.5 cm/1 inch piece of cinnamon stick
750 g/1½ lb boned leg of lamb, cubed
6 shallots, chopped
2 garlic cloves, finely chopped
5 cm/2 inch piece of fresh root ginger, chopped
2 tablespoons ground coriander seeds
2 teaspoons ground cumin seeds
1 teaspoon chilli powder
150 g/5 oz natural yogurt
1 teaspoon garam masala
salt
2 tablespoons finely chopped fresh coriander leaves, to garnish (optional)

heat 4 tablespoons of the oil in a pan, add the cardamoms, cloves, peppercorns and cinnamon and fry for 1 minute.

add the lamb, a few pieces at a time, and fry well to brown all over; transfer to a dish. Remove the whole spices and discard.

add the remaining oil to the pan and fry the shallots, garlic and ginger for 5 minutes, then add the coriander and cumin seeds, chilli powder, and salt to taste and cook for 5 minutes, stirring to avoid burning. Gradually stir in the yogurt until it is all absorbed.

return the meat to the pan with any liquid collected in the dish and add sufficient water just to cover the meat. Bring to simmering point, cover and cook for about 1 hour or until the meat is tender.

sprinkle on the garam masala and cook, stirring, for 1 minute. Garnish with chopped coriander, if liked, before serving.

Serves 4
Preparation time: *25 minutes*
Cooking time: *1½ hours*

Raan

2.5 kg/5 lb leg of lamb, skin and fat removed
50 g/2 oz fresh root ginger, chopped
6 garlic cloves, peeled
rind of 1 lemon
8 tablespoons lemon juice
2 teaspoons cumin seeds
6 cardamoms, peeled
1 teaspoon ground cloves
1 teaspoon turmeric
1½ teaspoons chilli powder
1 tablespoon salt
2 x 150 g/5 oz cartons natural yogurt
150 g/5 oz whole unpeeled almonds
4 tablespoons brown sugar
1 teaspoon saffron threads, soaked in 3 tablespoons boiling water
flatleaf parsley, to garnish

prick the lamb all over with a fork and make about 12 deep cuts.

blend the ginger, garlic, lemon rind and juice, spices and salt in a blender or food processor. Spread over the lamb and leave to stand for 1 hour in a flameproof casserole.

combine 4 tablespoons of the yogurt with the almonds and 2 tablespoons of the sugar. Stir in the remaining yogurt and pour over the lamb. Cover tightly and leave for 48 hours in the refrigerator.

allow the meat to return to room temperature. Sprinkle over the remaining sugar and cook, uncovered, in a preheated hot oven, 220°C/425°F/Gas Mark 7, for 30 minutes. Cover, lower the temperature to 160°C/325°F/Gas Mark 3 and cook for 3 hours, basting occasionally. Sprinkle the saffron water over the meat and cook for a further 30 minutes or until very tender.

remove the meat from the pan, wrap it in foil and keep warm. Skim off the fat from the casserole and boil the sauce until thick. Place the meat on a dish and pour over the sauce. Carve in thick slices to serve and garnish with parsley sprigs.

Serves 6
Preparation time: *20 minutes*, plus 1 hour
  standing time, plus 48 hours marinating time
Cooking time: *about 4 hours*
Oven temperature: 220°C/425°F/Gas Mark 7,
  then 160°C/325°F/Gas Mark 3

clipboard: Cloves are the immature, unopened flowerbuds of an evergreen tree that grows near the coast of tropical areas of southeast Asia, east Africa and the West Indies. They can be bought whole or ground, and are often used in India in meat and rice dishes.

Lamb Dhansak

Dhansak is a Parsee dish from western India, traditionally served on special occasions.

50 g/2 oz each red lentils, chickpeas and moong dhal
750 g/1½ lb lamb fillet, cut into 5 cm/2 inch cubes
300 g/10 oz aubergine, cubed
250 g/8 oz pumpkin, peeled and cubed
125 g/4 oz potato, peeled and cubed
2 onions, roughly chopped
2 tomatoes, skinned and chopped
75 g/3 oz fresh spinach, washed
3 tablespoons ghee or vegetable oil
1 large onion, thinly sliced
2 tablespoons tomato purée
salt
freshly ground black pepper
deep-fried onion slices, to garnish

Masala mixture
3 fresh red chillies, deseeded and chopped
3 fresh green chillies, deseeded and chopped
6 garlic cloves, crushed
2.5 cm/1 inch piece of fresh root ginger, finely chopped
25 g/1 oz fresh coriander leaves
15 g/½ oz fresh mint leaves
4 tablespoons water

Dry spice mixture
2 teaspoons turmeric
1 teaspoon black mustard seeds
½ teaspoon ground cinnamon
¼ teaspoon fenugreek powder
2 tablespoons dhana jeera powder
4 cardamoms, crushed

wash the lentils, chickpeas and moong dhal. Soak overnight in cold water.

drain the pulses the next day, and place in a large saucepan with the lamb. Pour over enough boiling water to cover the lentils and meat and season generously with salt. Bring to the boil, skim any scum from the surface, then cover and simmer, stirring occasionally, for about 20 minutes.

tip all the prepared vegetables into the pan, stir and continue cooking for a further 40 minutes, until the lentils and vegetables are cooked and the lamb is tender. Drain the liquid from the pan and remove the pieces of meat with a slotted spoon. Set the meat aside and tip the vegetables and lentils into a blender or food processor. Blend to a thick purée.

heat the ghee or oil in a large heavy-bottomed sauté pan and fry the onion over a gentle heat for 5 minutes, until it is softened and golden.

place all the masala ingredients in a food processor and blend to a paste. Add this paste to the softened onion and cook gently for a further 3 minutes. Stir in the dry spice mixture and cook, stirring, for 3 minutes.

add the lamb and vegetable purée to the pan, with the tomato purée and water. Season, cover and simmer for 30 minutes until thick. If it becomes too dry, add a little more water. Taste and adjust seasoning if necessary.

transfer to serving dish, garnish with fried onions and serve with rice.

Serves 6
Preparation time: *30 minutes*, plus overnight soaking time
Cooking time: *1¾ hours*

Balti Lamb Madras

with tomatoes and coconut flakes

1 tablespoon vegetable oil
1 onion, chopped
2 garlic cloves, crushed
2 fresh green chillies, deseeded and sliced
2 teaspoons chilli powder
2 teaspoons garam masala
500 g/1 lb lean lamb, cut into 3.5 cm/1½ inch cubes
1 tablespoon vinegar
1 teaspoon salt
2 tomatoes, skinned, deseeded and chopped
1 tablespoon coconut flakes, to garnish

heat the oil in a wok or heavy-bottomed frying pan and stir-fry the onion, garlic, chillies and chilli powder for 2 minutes. Add the garam masala, lamb, vinegar, salt and chopped tomatoes. Stir the mixture thoroughly.

cover the wok and cook for 30–40 minutes over a moderate heat until the lamb is tender, adding a little water if it appears to be sticking to the bottom of the wok.

transfer to a heated serving dish, scatter with the coconut flakes and serve immediately.

Serves 4
Preparation time: *10 minutes*
Cooking time: *35–45 minutes*

clipboard: Garam masala is a speciality from northern India, and varies from one region to another. It is generally a mild, sweet seasoning, and is available in many supermarkets and Indian food stores. The mixture usually consists of cardamom, cinnamon, cloves, cumin, coriander and black peppercorns. Optional extras may include nutmeg, mace and bay leaves.

Pork Vindaloo

This powerful pork curry is just the thing for devoted fans of spicy food. It owes some of its kick to a combination of spices, including mustard seeds, and to the addition of vinegar.

1–2 teaspoons chilli powder

1 teaspoon turmeric

2 teaspoons ground cumin seeds

2 teaspoons ground mustard seeds

2 tablespoons ground coriander seeds

3.5 cm/1½ inch piece of fresh root ginger, finely chopped

150 ml/¼ pint vinegar

1 large onion, finely chopped

2 garlic cloves, crushed

750 g/1½ lb pork fillet, cubed

4 tablespoons oil

salt

mix the spices, and salt to taste, with the vinegar. Put the onion, garlic, and pork in a bowl, pour over the vinegar mixture, cover and leave in the refrigerator overnight.

heat the oil in a large saucepan, add the pork mixture, bring to simmering point, cover and cook for about 45 minutes or until the pork is tender.

Serves 4
Preparation time: *10 minutes*, plus
  overnight marinating time
Cooking time: *55 minutes*

clipboard: Black and brown mustard is a native of India and is often used in Indian cooking – either in the form of whole seeds, which are heated in oil until they splutter, or ground, as in this recipe.

Bhuna Ghosht
with coriander and lemon

750 g/1½ lb pork fillets
2 tablespoons coriander seeds, roughly pounded
1 teaspoon freshly ground black pepper
1 tablespoon paprika
4 tablespoons oil
salt
2 tablespoons finely chopped fresh coriander leaves, to garnish
lemon wedges, to serve

slit the fillets lengthways and cut each side into quarters. Prick the pieces all over with a fork. Mix together the coriander, pepper, paprika and salt to taste and rub into the meat on both sides. Leave to stand for 1 hour.

heat the oil in a pan, add the meat and fry quickly on both sides to seal. Lower the heat and sauté for 5 minutes or until cooked through, stirring and turning to prevent burning.

sprinkle with the chopped coriander and serve with wedges of lemon.

Serves 4
Preparation time: *10 minutes*, plus
1 hour standing time
Cooking time: *10 minutes*

clipboard: Coriander seeds can be roughly pounded using a pestle and mortar, which consists of a bowl with a pounding tool. These are available in wood, ceramic or marble, and the inner surface should be rough, not smooth.

Beef

Meatball Curry

500 g/1 lb minced beef
2 large onions, chopped
4 garlic cloves, crushed
2 teaspoons turmeric
2 teaspoons chilli powder
2 teaspoons ground coriander
1½ teaspoons ground cumin
1 teaspoon ground ginger
2 teaspoons salt
1 egg, beaten
vegetable oil for deep-frying
125 g/4 oz ghee or 2 tablespoons vegetable oil
200 ml/7 fl oz water
mint or coriander leaves, to garnish

put the minced beef in a bowl with half of the onions, garlic, spices and salt. Stir well and then bind the mixture together with the beaten egg.

divide the minced beef mixture into 12 equal-sized portions and, using your hands, shape each one into a small ball.

heat the oil in a heavy-based saucepan until it is very hot. Add the meatballs in batches and deep-fry for 5 minutes. Remove and drain on absorbent kitchen paper and then set aside.

heat the ghee or vegetable oil in a large saucepan, add the remaining onions and garlic and fry gently for 4–5 minutes until soft. Add the remaining spices and salt and fry for 3 minutes, stirring constantly. Add the meatballs and coat them in the spices. Add the water and bring to the boil. Lower the heat and simmer gently for 30 minutes. Serve garnished with mint or coriander leaves.

Serves 4
Preparation time: *30 minutes*
Cooking time: *40 minutes*

Calcutta Beef Curry

This beef curry is a rich and hearty dish and is unusual in that it is simmered for a long time in a mixture of milk and spices until the meat is tender and the sauce well reduced.

1 teaspoon salt

1 tablespoon chilli powder

2 teaspoons ground coriander

1 teaspoon freshly ground black pepper

1½ teaspoons turmeric

1 teaspoon ground cumin

1 litre/1¾ pints milk

1 kg/2 lb braising steak, trimmed of fat and cut into 3.5 cm/1½ inch cubes

125 g/4 oz ghee or 2 tablespoons vegetable oil

2 large onions, thinly sliced

5 garlic cloves, thinly sliced

7 cm/3 inch piece of fresh root ginger, peeled and thinly sliced

2 teaspoons garam masala

put the salt and ground spices, except the garam masala, in a large bowl. Mix in the milk, a little at a time.

add the cubes of beef to the bowl and turn in the milk and spice mixture until they are evenly coated.

heat the ghee or vegetable oil in a large, heavy-based saucepan, add the onions, garlic and ginger and fry gently for 4–5 minutes until soft. Remove the cubes of beef from the milk and spice mixture and add to the saucepan. Fry gently over a moderate heat, turning constantly until the meat is evenly browned.

increase the heat, add the milk and spice mixture and bring to the boil. Cover the pan, reduce the heat and cook gently for 1½–2 hours until the beef is tender and the sauce reduced. Just before serving, add the garam masala and boil off any excess liquid to make a thick sauce.

Serves 6
Preparation time: *15 minutes*
Cooking time: *1¾–2¼ hours*

Spicy Beef in Yogurt

Hot and spicy, this beef curry has some of the heat taken out of it by the yogurt. Marinating and slow cooking make it both tender and succulent.

500 g/1 lb braising or stewing steak, finely sliced
1 teaspoon salt
300 ml/½ pint natural yogurt
175 g/6 oz ghee or 3 tablespoons vegetable oil
1 large onion, sliced
3 garlic cloves, sliced
1½ teaspoons ground ginger
2 teaspoons ground coriander
2 teaspoons chilli powder
½ teaspoon ground cumin
1½ teaspoons turmeric
1 teaspoon garam masala

place the beef between 2 sheets of greaseproof paper and beat until thin with a rolling pin or mallet.

rub the beef with the salt and then cut into serving-sized pieces. Place in a bowl and cover with the yogurt. Cover and leave to marinate overnight in the refrigerator.

heat the ghee or vegetable oil in a heavy-based saucepan and add the onion and garlic. Fry gently for 4–5 minutes until soft. Add the spices and fry for a further 3 minutes, stirring constantly.

add the beef and yogurt marinade to the pan and stir well. Cover the pan with a tightly fitting lid and then simmer for 1½ hours, or until the meat is tender. Serve with rice.

Serves 4
Preparation time: *15 minutes*, plus
  overnight marinating time
Cooking time: *1¾ hours*

Beef Buffad

Cook cubed braising steak slowly with a subtle combination of spices and coconut milk until the meat is tender and succulent, and the sauce is rich and thick.

3 tablespoons oil
2 onions, sliced
2 garlic cloves, finely chopped
3 fresh green chillies, chopped
3.5 cm/1½ inch piece of fresh root ginger, chopped
750 g/1½ lb braising steak, cubed
½ teaspoon chilli powder
1 teaspoon turmeric
1 teaspoon freshly ground black pepper
1 teaspoon ground cumin seeds
1 tablespoon ground coriander seeds
½ teaspoon ground cinnamon
½ teaspoon ground cloves
300 ml/½ pint coconut milk
150 ml/¼ pint vinegar
salt

heat the oil in a large saucepan, add the onions and fry until they are just beginning to brown, then add the garlic, chillies and ginger. Fry for 1 minute, then add the beef and remaining spices. Stir well and cook for 5 minutes, stirring occasionally.

add the coconut milk, which should just cover the meat; if it does not, add a little water. Add salt to taste. Bring to simmering point, cover and cook for about 1½ hours, until the meat is almost tender.

stir in the vinegar and continue cooking for about 30 minutes until the meat is tender and the gravy is thick.

Serves 4
Preparation time: *30 minutes*
Cooking time: *2 hours*

clipboard: If you can't find any coconut milk, you can use 75 g/3 oz creamed coconut melted in 250 ml/8 fl oz warm water instead. Creamed coconut is sold in blocks, which should always be softened in warm water before use.

Stuffed Peppers
with beef, rice and tomatoes

5 tablespoons oil
1 onion, finely chopped
2 teaspoons ground coriander seeds
1 teaspoon ground cumin seeds
½ teaspoon chilli powder
375 g/12 oz minced beef
3 tablespoons long-grain rice
4 large green or red peppers
1 x 425 g/14 oz can tomatoes
salt

heat 3 tablespoons of the oil in a saucepan, add the onion and fry until golden. Add the spices and cook for 2 minutes. Add the minced beef and fry, stirring, until browned. Add the rice and salt to taste and cook for 2 minutes. Remove from the heat and leave to cool.

slice the peppers lengthways and discard the seeds and cores. Fill the pepper shells with the meat mixture.

pour the remaining oil into a pan just large enough to hold the peppers. Heat the oil and place the peppers in the pan. Pour a little of the canned tomato juice into each pepper and the remaining juice and tomatoes into the pan, seasoning with salt to taste. Bring to simmering point, cover and cook for about 25 minutes until the rice is tender.

Serves 4
Preparation time: *35 minutes*
Cooking time: *30 minutes*

clipboard: A variation of this recipe using lamb instead of beef is also delicious, especially if you use succulent spring lamb.

Rice, grains and pulses

Chickpeas

Brown Basmati rice

Wholemeal flour

Sprouted mung beans

Chickpeas

These are small pea-shaped seeds, which are pale golden in colour and have a pleasantly nutty flavour. They are often used in stews or soups, and are also boiled and ground to a paste to make hummus. Chickpeas are used to make a special flour, known as besan. This is a very fine yellow flour used in bread cookery. The chick peas are ground very finely. The flour should be sieved before use as it tends to form hard lumps during storage. It is very low in gluten. Chickpeas can also be roasted, covered in spices and served as a savoury snack.

Wholemeal flour

Wholemeal flour is a coarse-textured flour which is used to make bread, cakes, biscuits and pasta, as well as chapatis, parathas and puris. Ordinary wholemeal flour – which should be very well sieved beforehand – may also be used to make Indian breads. The flour is made by grinding the wheat kernel, which includes the bran, germ or embryo, and endosperm. It has a high fibre content and is therefore healthier than white flour.

Brown Basmati rice

Apart from wheat, rice is the most widely cultivated cereal in the world. India is one of the largest consumers of rice worldwide. Basmati rice is an Indian rice, with very small, round grains and a distinctive flavour. Brown Basmati rice is wholegrain rice with only the outer husk removed, leaving the bran layers, and therefore has a characteristic beige colour. It is more nutritious than white rice because, as only the outer husk has been removed, it retains some of the B vitamins, phosphorus and starch. It is also high in fibre. It has a rather more nutty flavour and more chewy texture than white rice, and is now becoming very popular in the West, largely because of the trend for a healthy, high-fibre diet. Always buy good quality Basmati rice, and soak it for 20–30 minutes before cooking, then drain well. Soaking prevents the rice sticking during the cooking process.

Sprouted mung beans

The mung bean is a bean plant, originating in the Far East. It is usually olive green in colour, though it may also

White Basmati rice

Gram flour

Masoor dhal

Dried moong dhal

sometimes be yellow or black, and is spherical in shape. It should be thoroughly boiled for about 15 minutes to destroy any harmful toxins. The mung bean is widely cultivated for its shoots, which are popularly known as bean sprouts and are delicious eaten either blanched or raw. Bean sprouts can be bought either fresh or canned from many shops specializing in Indian and Asian foods, as well as in many good supermarkets.

White Basmati rice
Basmati rice is a rice native to Asia, which has been grown for thousands of years and is widely associated with Indian cuisine. White Basmati rice is brown rice from which the germ and the outer layers have been removed by passing the grains through machines that rasp the grain. It has a more bland flavour than brown rice and is less nutritionally valuable, but it is nevertheless popular and widely used.

Masoor dhal
Masoor dhal is a small, round, dried red lentil, which has been husked and split. These split lentils should be cooked and added to dishes, or can be cooked with garlic, onion and Indian spices as a dish in their own right. They are widely available in most supermarkets, and are labelled simply 'lentils' or 'red lentils'. Lentils are nourishing and have a high energy content. They are particularly rich in protein,

carbohydrates, phosphorus and iron, as well as the B vitamins. Red lentils do not need to be soaked before cooking as they cook quickly without soaking.

Gram flour
This flour made from lentils, is used in India to thicken sauces, in curry powder and to make pakoras. It is finely milled to a light golden colour and has a distinctive taste. Gram flour is also very useful for people who are allergic to

gluten, a component of all wheat products. You can make your own substitute by finely grinding yellow split peas.

Moong dhal
Moong dhal is a dried whole or split yellow bean, which is tear drop-shaped and has a green skin and yellow flesh. It also has a white stripe where the bean was attached to the pod. The beans are used in soups. They are more popular in northern India than in the south.

Chilli Fry
with pepper and tomatoes

4 tablespoons oil

1 large onion, finely chopped

½ teaspoon ground coriander seeds

½ teaspoon turmeric

2.5 cm/1 inch piece of fresh root ginger, finely chopped

1 chilli, chopped

500 g/1 lb frying steak, cut into strips about 2.5 x 1 cm/1 x ½ inch thick

1 green or red pepper, cored, deseeded and roughly chopped

2 tomatoes, quartered

4 tablespoons lemon juice

salt

lemon wedges, to garnish

heat the oil in a lidded frying pan, add the onion and fry until soft. Add the coriander, turmeric, ginger and chilli and fry over a low heat for 5 minutes; if the mixture becomes dry, add 1 tablespoon water.

add the strips of steak, increase the heat and cook, stirring, until browned all over. Add the chopped pepper, cover and simmer gently for 5–10 minutes, until the meat is tender. Add the tomatoes, lemon juice and salt to taste and cook, uncovered, for 2–3 minutes. (This dish should be rather dry.) Serve, garnished with lemon wedges, if liked.

Serves 4
Preparation time: *5 minutes*
Cooking time: *35 minutes*

clipboard: Many Indian recipes require finely chopped ginger root. Here is a useful technique for doing this. Peel the piece of root ginger, and trim both ends flat. Stand on one end, and make a line of vertical cuts with a sharp knife. Holding the cut root together, turn it at right angles. Cut through again, making lines of fine strips. These can then be neatly chopped into small squares.

Aloo Cakes

Aloo is the Indian word for potato, which was not introduced to India until the 16th century.

3 tablespoons oil
I large onion, finely chopped
I cm/½ inch piece of fresh root ginger, finely chopped
I teaspoon ground coriander seeds
250 g/8 oz minced beef
I tablespoon raisins
I tablespoon finely chopped fresh coriander leaves
I kg/2 lb potatoes, boiled and mashed with a little milk and salt
flour for coating
oil for shallow-frying
salt
½ red pepper, sliced into strips
½ yellow pepper, sliced into strips
I inch/2.5 cm mooli (winter radish) or a few radishes, very thinly sliced

heat the oil in a frying pan, add the onion and ginger and fry until golden. Add the ground coriander and minced beef and fry until brown.

add the raisins and salt to taste and simmer for about 20 minutes, until the meat is cooked. Spoon out any fat in the pan. Stir in the chopped coriander and leave to cool.

divide the mashed potato into 8 portions. With well-floured hands, flatten each portion on one palm, put 3 teaspoons of the meat mixture in the centre of each and fold the potato over to cover. Form gently into a round patty shape.

dip the potato cakes lightly in flour and shallow-fry a few at a time in hot oil, until crisp and golden, turning carefully to brown the underside.

serve with strips of red and yellow pepper and very thin slices of mooli or radish, if liked.

Serves 4
Preparation time: *1 hour*
Cooking time: *15 minutes*

Kofta in Yogurt

Spicy meatballs are fried until golden brown and crisp, and served with natural yogurt and chopped coriander.

500 g/1 lb minced beef

75 g/3 oz fresh breadcrumbs

2 fresh green chillies, finely chopped

1 onion, finely chopped

2.5 cm/1 inch piece of fresh root ginger, finely chopped

2 teaspoons ground coriander seeds

1 egg, lightly beaten

oil for frying

500 g/1 lb natural yogurt

salt

2 tablespoons finely chopped fresh coriander leaves, to garnish

mix together the minced beef, breadcrumbs, chillies, onion, ginger, ground coriander, salt to taste and egg, and shape the mixture into walnut-sized balls.

heat the oil in a large pan, add the meatballs and fry until well browned and cooked through. Drain carefully.

pour the yogurt into a serving bowl and add the meatballs while still hot. Sprinkle with chopped coriander and serve warm.

Serves 4
Preparation time: *15 minutes*
Cooking time: *15 minutes*

clipboard: Chop coriander finely without cutting your fingers by using a mezzaluna, which you operate with a rocking motion until your herbs are chopped finely enough.

Balti Beef and Broccoli

with onion and chopped tomatoes

50 g/2 oz ghee or vegetable oil
1 large onion, chopped
2 garlic cloves, crushed
500 g/1 lb frying steak, cut into narrow strips
1 tablespoon ground coriander
1 teaspoon garam masala
1 teaspoon chilli powder
1 teaspoon mustard powder
1 x 250 g/8 oz can chopped tomatoes
250 g/8 oz broccoli, washed and separated into florets, stalks sliced
salt

melt the ghee or vegetable oil in a heavy-based frying pan and fry the onion until lightly browned. Add the garlic and fry for 1 minute further.

add the steak, increase the heat and stir-fry until the steak is browned on all sides. Lower the heat, then cover and cook the meat in its own juices until tender, about 10 minutes.

stir in the coriander, garam masala, chilli, mustard and a pinch of salt and stir-fry over a low heat for a few seconds. Stir in the canned chopped tomatoes and juice and cook, uncovered, until almost dry. Add the broccoli and stir-fry for a few minutes. Partly cover the frying pan and simmer until tender, then serve at once.

Serves 4
Preparation time: *20 minutes*
Cooking time: *30 minutes*

clipboard: Chilli powder varies according to its country of origin. Indian chilli powder is made from the dried and ground flesh and seeds of red chillies and adds the hottest element to curry powder. It is very similar to cayenne pepper and the two can be used interchangeably.

Vegetarian

Fried Chilli Cabbage

with potatoes, peas and carrots

125 g/4 oz ghee or 2 tablespoons vegetable oil

1 small onion, chopped

6 garlic cloves, crushed

1 teaspoon white cumin seeds

1 teaspoon turmeric

1 white cabbage, coarsely chopped

125 g/4 oz potatoes, peeled and chopped

125 g/4 oz shelled peas

125 g/4 oz carrots, sliced

250 g/8 oz tomatoes, skinned and sliced

1 teaspoon green mango powder

1 fresh green chilli, chopped

15 g/½ oz fresh root ginger, grated

1 teaspoon garam masala

1 tablespoon chopped fresh coriander leaves

2 tablespoons melted butter, to serve

heat the ghee or vegetable oil in a large saucepan and fry the onion and garlic with the cumin seeds for about 5 minutes until golden brown. Add the turmeric and shake the pan for a few seconds.

add the cabbage, potatoes, peas and carrots. Cook, stirring continuously, for 5 minutes. Cover the pan and continue to cook gently over a low heat for a further 10 minutes.

stir in the tomatoes, green mango powder, chilli and ginger. Stir well and then replace the lid and continue cooking for 10 more minutes.

sprinkle the garam masala and chopped coriander into the saucepan and stir well. Heat through over a low heat for about 5 minutes. Serve hot with the melted butter poured over the top.

Serves 4–6
Preparation time: *20 minutes*
Cooking time: *35 minutes*

clipboard: White cumin seeds have a similar, slightly sweetish aniseed flavour to fennel seeds

Cauliflower Curry

125 g/4 oz ghee or 2 tablespoons vegetable oil

pinch of asafoetida powder

750 g/1½ lb cauliflower, cut into florets

300 ml/½ pint natural yogurt

2 large onions, finely chopped

2 garlic cloves, crushed

4 bay leaves

300 ml/½ pint hot water

salt

Spices

6 cloves

6 black peppercorns

1 black cardamom

2 green cardamoms

2 x 2.5 cm/1 inch pieces of cinnamon stick

1 teaspoon coriander seeds

1 teaspoon white cumin seeds

1 teaspoon red chilli powder

heat 25 g/1 oz of the ghee or ½ teaspoon of vegetable oil in a large saucepan with the asafoetida. Add the cauliflower and cook over a medium heat for 5 minutes. Using a slotted spoon, transfer the cauliflower to a bowl and pour the yogurt over the top.

add the remaining ghee or vegetable oil to the pan and when it is hot, add the onions, garlic, salt to taste, bay leaves and all the spices except the chilli powder. Fry until the onions are golden and soft and then stir in the chilli powder.

return the cauliflower and yogurt to the pan and stir gently to combine all the ingredients. Cook gently over a low heat for 10 minutes.

pour in the hot water and simmer, stirring occasionally, for 25 minutes or until the cauliflower is tender. Serve this curry hot.

Serves 4–6
Preparation time: *15 minutes*
Cooking time: *45 minutes*

clipboard: Asafoetida powder is formed from the sap that flows from the roots of a large plant which grows in India and looks a little like cow parsley. The roots are cut with a knife in early summer and the milky sap that seeps out of them turns into a hard, resin-like substance. This is then sold either in block form or ground into powder. Be careful to store it in an airtight container, as it has a strong and unpleasant smell. Luckily, this disappears on contact with heat, when a subtle oniony flavour develops. It is highly prized by members of certain Indian sects who are not allowed to eat onions. Use in small quantities.

Spinach with Tomatoes

Rich in both colour and flavour, this delicious vegetable dish combines spinach with tomatoes, onions and spices.

1 kg/2 lb fresh spinach

175 g/6 oz ghee or 3 tablespoons vegetable oil

2 large onions, thinly sliced

2 garlic cloves, thinly sliced

150 g/5 oz piece of fresh root ginger, peeled and cut into strips 3 mm/⅛ inch thick

2 teaspoons chilli powder

2 teaspoons turmeric

2 teaspoons garam masala

2 teaspoons coriander seeds

1 teaspoon ground coriander

1 teaspoon cumin seeds

1½ teaspoons salt

2 teaspoons freshly ground black pepper

1 x 425 g/14 oz can tomatoes

wash the spinach thoroughly and then shake it dry. Remove any thick stalks and cut the spinach leaves into strips, about 2.5 cm/1 inch wide.

heat the ghee or vegetable oil in a large, heavy-based saucepan and add the onions and garlic. Fry gently over a moderate heat for about 5 minutes until they are golden and soft.

add the ginger to the pan and cook gently for 5–6 minutes. Stir in the chilli powder, turmeric, garam masala, coriander seeds, ground coriander, cumin seeds, salt and pepper and cook for 1 minute.

toss in the spinach and mix well to coat in the spice mixture. Add the tomatoes with their juice and bring to the boil, stirring. Add enough boiling water to prevent the spinach sticking to the bottom of the pan. Simmer for 5–10 minutes until the spinach and tomatoes are cooked.

Serves 4–6
Preparation time: *15 minutes*
Cooking time: *20–25 minutes*

Stuffed Aubergines

4–6 aubergines, halved lengthways

100 ml/3½ fl oz water

1 bay leaf

125 g/4 oz ghee or 2 tablespoons vegetable oil

1 large onion, finely chopped

2 garlic cloves, finely chopped

2 teaspoons coriander seeds

1 teaspoon chilli powder

1 teaspoon lovage seeds (optional)

1 teaspoon salt

To garnish

fresh coriander leaves

dried red chillies, chopped

place the aubergines in a roasting pan with the cut sides upwards. Pour in the water, add the bay leaf and cover the pan tightly with foil. Poach in a preheated oven at 160°C/325°F/Gas Mark 3 for 25 minutes or until soft.

heat the ghee or vegetable oil in a heavy-based saucepan and gently fry the onion and garlic for 4–5 minutes until soft. Crush the coriander seeds coarsely and add to the onion mixture with the chilli powder, lovage seeds, if using, and salt. Stir well and fry for 2–3 minutes.

remove the poached aubergines from the water and pat dry with absorbent kitchen paper. With a teaspoon, scrape out the flesh, reserving the skins. Mash the flesh and add to the spice mixture. Fry for 2–3 minutes, stirring.

grill the aubergine skins for 5 minutes until dried out, and fill with the fried mixture. Arrange on a serving dish and serve garnished with coriander leaves and chillies.

Serves 4–6
Preparation time: *20 minutes*
Cooking time: *35 minutes*
Oven temperature:
  160°C/325°F/Gas Mark 3

clipboard: Lovage is an aromatic herb, originally from Persia. The leaves taste rather like celery, and the seeds can also be used and go particularly well with vegetables. The leaf stalks can be candied, rather like angelica.

Cream Cheese Kofta Curry

1 kg/2 lb potatoes, quartered

1 large fresh green chilli, chopped

1 teaspoon peeled and grated fresh root ginger

½ teaspoon garam masala

2 tablespoons chickpea or gram flour

2 tablespoons fresh breadcrumbs

1 tablespoon roasted coriander seeds, ground

250 g/8 oz panir

1 tablespoon grated or desiccated coconut

1 egg white, beaten

175 g/6 oz ghee or 3 tablespoons vegetable oil

2 bay leaves

2 onions, chopped

6 garlic cloves, crushed

4 cloves

6 black peppercorns

150 ml/¼ pint natural yogurt

1 teaspoon turmeric

1 teaspoon chilli powder

300 ml/½ pint water

500 g/1 lb tomatoes, skinned and sliced

2 tablespoons chopped fresh coriander leaves

salt

boil the potatoes in some water with the green chilli, ginger and all but a pinch of the garam masala. When tender, drain the potatoes and mash with a little salt, the chickpea or gram flour, breadcrumbs and coriander. Divide into 12 equal-sized portions.

mix the panir with the coconut and the remaining garam masala. Divide into 12 equal-sized portions. Flatten the potato portions and use to wrap around the panir portions. Roll into balls, brush with beaten egg white and fry in the heated ghee or oil until golden brown. Drain and transfer to an ovenproof dish.

add the bay leaves, onions, garlic, cloves and peppercorns to the ghee or oil left in the pan and fry until golden. Stir in the yogurt, turmeric and chilli powder. Add the water and bring to the boil. Simmer for 10 minutes.

pour this sauce over the koftas and cover with the tomatoes and coriander leaves. Cook in a preheated oven at 180°C/350°F/Gas Mark 4 for 10–15 minutes, or until heated through. Serve immediately.

Serves 4–6
Preparation time: *30 minutes*
Cooking time: *1 hour*
Oven temperature:
   180C/350F/Gas Mark 4

clipboard: To skin a tomato, put it in a bowl, pour boiling water on to it and leave for 2–3 minutes. Remove the tomato, pierce the skin with the point of a knife, and the skin will then come away easily.

Vegetable Rolls

with quick chutney

5 potatoes, boiled and coarsely mashed

2 tablespoons chopped fresh coriander leaves

2 fresh green chillies, deseeded and chopped

2 teaspoons lime juice

1 teaspoon garam masala

oil for deep-frying

salt and freshly ground black pepper

Quick chutney

1 large bunch of fresh coriander leaves

3 fresh green chillies, deseeded and chopped

1 teaspoon sugar

½ teaspoon salt

3 tablespoons grated fresh coconut

juice of ½ lime

Batters

50 g/2 oz chickpea or gram flour (besan)

175 g/6 oz plain flour

300 ml/½ pint water

pinch of chilli powder

1 teaspoon baking powder

300 ml/½ pint milk

ghee or vegetable oil for frying

salt

To serve

1 small onion, chopped

1 carrot, grated

¼ crisp lettuce, shredded

start by making the quick chutney: trim the stalks from the coriander and grind the leaves with the chillies, sugar, salt, coconut and lime juice to form a paste. You can do this either by pounding in a mortar or by grinding in a blender or food processor. Put to one side.

prepare the filling for the pancake rolls: mix together the potatoes, coriander, chillies, lime juice, garam masala, salt and pepper. Shape the mixture into rolls, about 2.5 cm/1 inch in diameter and 10 cm/4 inches in length. Set aside.

make the two batters: mix the chickpea or gram flour with 50 g/2 oz of the plain flour and beat in the water to make a batter for the potato rolls. Add the salt and chilli powder and set aside. Mix the remaining plain flour with the baking powder and a pinch of salt. Beat in the milk to make a smooth pancake batter.

heat a little ghee or vegetable oil in a small frying pan and pour in some batter, swirl it around the pan to form a thick pancake. Cook until browned underneath, flip over and cook the other side. Repeat with the remaining batter. Layer the pancakes with kitchen paper and keep warm.

heat the oil for deep-frying to 180°C/350°F. Dip the potato rolls in the prepared water batter and then deep-fry, a few at a time until golden. Remove and drain. Spread each pancake with a little of the prepared chutney and then top with a potato roll and some onion, carrot and lettuce. Fold over and serve.

Serves 6
Preparation time: *40 minutes*
Cooking time: *10–15 minutes*

Spicy Okra

This mild curry made with fresh okra, or ladies' fingers, and tomatoes is both flavoured and garnished with fresh mint.

2 large onions, peeled
125 g/4 oz ghee or 2 tablespoons vegetable oil
4 garlic cloves
2 teaspoons ground coriander
½ teaspoon turmeric
500 g/1 lb fresh okra, topped and tailed and cut into
1 cm/½ inch slices
2 tomatoes, skinned and chopped
1 teaspoon chopped fresh mint
½ teaspoon garam masala
salt and freshly ground black pepper
fresh mint, to garnish

slice one of the onions very thinly. Heat the ghee or vegetable oil in a heavy-based saucepan and add the sliced onion. Fry gently until tender and golden brown.

chop the remaining onion and place in a blender or food processor with the garlic, seasoning, coriander and turmeric. Process until the mixture is well blended.

stir the blended onion and spice mixture into the fried onion in the saucepan and cook over a medium heat for 5 minutes, stirring occasionally.

add the okra to the saucepan. Stir gently and then simmer, covered, for 20 minutes. Add the tomatoes, chopped mint and garam masala and simmer for 15 minutes. Serve garnished with fresh mint.

Serves 4
Preparation time: *10 minutes*
Cooking time: *45 minutes*

clipboard: Okra is a tropical plant grown for its pods, which have longitudinal ridges and under-ripe seeds inside them. Okra can be bought from most large supermarkets all year round and is also available dried and in cans. They are particularly rich in calcium, phosphorus, iron and vitamin C.

Phul Gobi
with green, yellow and red peppers

3 tablespoons oil
1 onion, sliced
½ teaspoon turmeric
1 cauliflower, broken into florets
2 fresh green chillies, deseeded
1 green pepper, cored, deseeded and cut into strips
1 yellow pepper, cored, deseeded and cut into strips
1 red pepper, cored, deseeded and cut into strips
salt

heat the oil in a pan, add the onion and fry until soft. Add the turmeric and cook for 1 minute. Add the cauliflower and salt to taste. Stir well, cover and cook gently for about 10 minutes until the cauliflower is almost cooked.

add the chillies and peppers, stir and cook for a further 5 minutes or until tender.

Serves 4
Preparation time: *5 minutes*
Cooking time: *25–30 minutes*

clipboard: The combination of green, yellow and red peppers in this recipe makes it a particularly attractive dish. The preparation time is a lot shorter than the cooking time, making it a quick and easy dish to add to your repertoire.

Vegetables, herbs and fruit

Bay leaves

Mango

Coconut

Ginger

Cayenne peppers

Bird's eye chilli peppers

Bay leaves

Bay is not a true herb but the leaf of the laurel tree. Because of its strong aroma, though, it is often treated as a herb. Traditionally, bay leaves were used in Roman times to crown victors in cultural or sporting events. Bay requires long slow cooking in order for the full flavour to develop.

Mango

The mango is a sweet tropical fruit, whose golden flesh is surrounded by smooth, red, yellow or green skin. It has a large single seed and can be eaten by itself or used in curries, chutneys or ice-cream. Mangoes are at their best in summer but are available canned all year round.

Cayenne peppers

Perhaps the best-known chilli pepper, although usually bought as cayenne pepper, which is made by crushing the dried pods.

Coconut

The coconut is a large nut, the fruit of the coconut palm, which grows in the tropics. The flesh of the coconut is white and rich in oil, and the nut also contains a translucent liquid. The soft pulp can be eaten by itself or incorporated in different forms in both sweet and savoury dishes. The liquid also makes a refreshing drink, which can be drunk by itself or mixed with alcohol.

Bird's eye chilli peppers

Also known as Mexican Peanuts, these tiny bead-like peppers measure just 5mm (¼ inch) across. Their small size belies their fiery taste, so they should only be used sparingly.

Ginger

Ginger is a brown, knobbly root, which has a pale golden flesh. It is used to flavour both sweet and savoury dishes and is used extensively in Indian cooking. The root must be peeled and finely chopped before being added to dishes. Ground ginger is often used in desserts. Ginger can also be pickled, preserved or crystallized.

Aubergine

The aubergine is sometimes known as eggplant because of its shape. It is, in fact, a fruit but is usually cooked and eaten as a vegetable. It has dark, smooth purple skin

Coriander

Curry leaves

Aubergine

Garlic

Jalapeño chillies

Okra

Mint

and pale greenish cream flesh. It can be steamed, boiled, grilled or sautéed.

Mint

Mint is a very fragrant herb with a strong fresh flavour. There are 25 different varieties of mint, all of which have bright green leaves and small white flowers. It is used extensively in many Indian dishes, especially with lamb. Fresh mint is a good garnish. It can also be dried.

Curry leaves

The small glossy evergreen curry leaves look similar to those of the bay tree. They should be used fresh or, if they are dried, as an ingredient in curry powder. Curry leaves may be chopped, crumbled, fried or powdered.

Garlic

Garlic is a bulb-shaped root vegetable. The bulb is arranged as a series of cloves which are wrapped in a papery white skin. Garlic has been in popular use for centuries, and has been a powerful ingredient in the history of cooking. It is also prized for its health-giving properties, being used to treat various ailments and ward off evil spirits. The pungent aroma and flavour of garlic adds character to any dish.

Coriander

Coriander is a member of the carrot family. It has bright green, lacy leaves, which have a strong aroma and flavour, and little white flowers. The leaves, roots and seeds are all used in cooking and it is used extensively in a great many Indian dishes. The leaves make a particularly attractive garnish.

Jalapeño chillies

A well-known, versatile chilli which can be either green or red. It is a fleshy, almost sausage-shaped fruit, 6–7 cm (2½–3) inches long and has a very hot taste.

Okra

Okra, also known as ladies' fingers, is a finger-sized green pod, pointed at one end, which contains small white seeds. It can be cooked whole or sliced and is popular in Indian cookery. It is gelatinous when cooked and can be used as a thickening agent. It is in season from summer through to autumn.

Panir Mattar

A combination of peas with curd cheese, this is a favourite vegetable dish in many Indian restaurants. Follow this recipe and you won't even need to go out to enjoy it.

2–3 tablespoons oil

125 g/4 oz panir (curd cheese), cut into 1 cm/½ inch cubes

2 tablespoons finely chopped onion

75 ml/3 fl oz water

250 g/8 oz shelled peas

½ teaspoon sugar

1 tablespoon grated fresh root ginger

2 fresh green chillies, finely chopped

½ teaspoon garam masala

1 tablespoon finely chopped fresh coriander

salt

heat the oil in a heavy-based pan, add the panir and fry until golden, turning gently and taking care not to burn it. Remove from the pan and set aside. Add the onions to the pan and fry until coloured; remove and set aside.

add the water, and salt to taste, to the pan and bring to the boil. Add the peas and sugar, cover and simmer until the peas are almost tender. If necessary, uncover and cook for 1 minute to evaporate any liquid.

return the onions to the pan, add the ginger and chillies and stir well. Cook for 2 minutes, then very gently stir in the panir. Heat through for 2 minutes, then stir in the garam masala and coriander. Serve immediately.

Serves 4
Preparation time: *5 minutes*
Cooking time: *25 minutes*

clipboard: Panir is an Indian curd cheese used in cooking. It is available from Indian specialist food stores. It goes particularly well with vegetable dishes made with peas or spinach.

Gram and Bean Dhal *with marrow and chilli*

1.2 litres/2 pints water
125 g/4 oz split grams or yellow split peas
125 g/4 oz dried beans
½ teaspoon turmeric
125 g/4 oz peeled and sliced marrow, cut into
5 cm/2 inch pieces
125 g/4 oz ghee or 2 tablespoons vegetable oil
1 onion, finely chopped
6 garlic cloves, crushed
1 teaspoon white cumin seeds
1 fresh green chilli, chopped
1 dried red chilli, crushed
½ teaspoon chilli powder
salt
fried onions, to garnish

bring the water to the boil in a large saucepan. Meanwhile, wash the grams or split peas and beans in a colander under cold running water and then drain well.

tip the drained grams and beans into the boiling water with a good pinch of salt and the turmeric. Bring the water back to the boil, cover the pan and simmer for 1½ hours, stirring occasionally.

add the marrow to the pan with the grams and beans. Simmer gently for a further 30 minutes.

heat the ghee or vegetable oil in a frying pan and fry the onion, garlic and cumin until golden brown. Remove from the heat and add the chillies and chilli powder.

serve the dhal hot with the fried onion sprinkled on top.

Serves 6
Preparation time: *15 minutes*
Cooking time: *2 hours*

Sprouting Mung Dhal

with fennel seeds and ginger

250 g/8 oz whole mung beans, rinsed
3–4 tablespoons oil
1 onion, thinly sliced
2 fresh green chillies, deseeded and chopped
2.5 cm/1 inch piece of fresh root ginger, cut into fine matchsticks
1 teaspoon fennel seeds
300 ml/½ pint water
salt

place the beans in a bowl a day before they are required, and barely cover them with warm water. Cover the bowl with clingfilm and leave in a warm dark place. Do not let the beans dry out; add a little extra water if necessary. The beans will have sprouted by the next day. Rinse and drain them.

heat the oil in a saucepan. Add the onion and fry, stirring, for 3 minutes. Stir in the chillies, ginger and fennel seeds and cook, stirring, until the onions have softened a little.

add the beans, salt to taste, and the water. Bring to simmering point, cover and cook gently, stirring occasionally, for 25–30 minutes or until the beans are soft and there is no liquid left.

Serves 4
Preparation time: *15 minutes*, plus
  overnight standing time
Cooking time: *30 minutes*

clipboard: Mung beans come from a bean plant, called haricot mungo, originating from the Far East, with small green yellow or brown seeds.

Aloo Sag

Potatoes and spinach are happy partners, whose flavours complement each other wonderfully in this delicious vegetarian dish.

6 tablespoons oil

1 onion, chopped

2.5 cm/1 inch piece of fresh root ginger, chopped

2 fresh green chillies, finely chopped

1 teaspoon turmeric

2 garlic cloves, finely chopped

500 g/1 lb potatoes, cut into small pieces

2 x 250 g/8 oz packets frozen spinach leaf, thawed

salt

heat the oil in a lidded frying pan, add the onion and cook until soft. Add the ginger, chillies, turmeric and garlic and cook for 5 minutes. Add the potatoes, and salt to taste, stir well, cover and cook for 10 minutes.

squeeze out any liquid from the spinach and chop. Add to the potatoes and cook for about 5 minutes, until both vegetables are tender.

Serves 4
Preparation time: *5 minutes*
Cooking time: *30 minutes*

clipboard: This recipe uses frozen spinach leaf, thawed, but you could equally well use fresh if you prefer, which would give both a slightly stronger colour and flavour.

Tamatar Aloo

An interesting way of cooking potatoes and tomatoes with spices and lemon juice, this is a fantastic vegetarian dish. Serve it either with other vegetables, or to accompany a meat dish.

2 tablespoons oil

½ teaspoon mustard seeds

250 g/8 oz potatoes, cut into small cubes

1 teaspoon turmeric

1 teaspoon chilli powder

2 teaspoons paprika

4 tablespoons lemon juice

1 teaspoon sugar

250 g/8 oz tomatoes, quartered

salt

2 tablespoons finely chopped coriander leaves, to garnish

heat the oil in a saucepan, add the mustard seeds and fry until they pop, this should only take a few seconds. Add the potatoes and fry for about 5 minutes. Add the spices, lemon juice, sugar and salt to taste, stir well and cook for 5 minutes.

add the tomatoes, stir well, then simmer for 5–10 minutes until the potatoes are tender. Serve garnished with coriander leaves.

Serves 4
Preparation time: *5 minutes*
Cooking time: *20 minutes*

clipboard: Turmeric is often regarded as a poor man's saffron – largely because it so much less expensive. It has a more bitter taste than saffron and is an ingredient in commercial curry powders. Be careful not to spill it as it stains clothing and work surfaces.

Bharta

This is definitely one of the most interesting dishes you can produce with aubergines — simple, quick, slightly spicy, and utterly delicious.

500 g/1 lb aubergines
2 tablespoons oil
1 large onion, finely chopped
1 garlic clove, crushed
1 fresh green chilli, deseeded and chopped
1 tablespoon ground coriander seeds
1 tablespoon finely chopped fresh coriander leaves, plus extra to garnish
1 tablespoon lemon juice
salt

cook the aubergines in a preheated moderate oven, 180°C/350°F/Gas Mark 4, for 30 minutes or until soft.

cool slightly, then slit open, scoop out all the aubergine flesh and mash it with a fork.

heat the oil in a pan, add the onion, garlic and chilli and fry until the onion is soft but not coloured.

add the ground and fresh coriander and salt to taste. Add the aubergine pulp, stir well and fry, uncovered, for 2 minutes, then cover and simmer very gently for 5 minutes. Sprinkle with lemon juice and serve, garnished with coriander leaves.

Serves 4
Preparation time: *40 minutes*
Cooking time: *20 minutes*
Oven temperature:
    180°C/350°F/Gas Mark 4

clipboard: Coriander is used extensively in Indian cooking, both as a spice and as a herb. The seeds have a warm fruity flavour and have been used for hundreds of years, while the leaves have only regained their popularity in recent years. Coriander seeds are equally good used either on their own or combined with other spices. They are one of the ingredients in commercial curry powder.

Kabli Channa

The only tricky thing about this recipe is remembering to soak the grams overnight. The rest is easy!

250 g/8 oz whole Bengal grams
750 ml/1¼ pints water
1 teaspoon salt
2 tablespoons ghee or vegetable oil
1 onion, chopped
2.5 cm/1 inch piece of cinnamon stick
4 cloves
2 garlic cloves, crushed
2.5 cm/1 inch piece of fresh root ginger, chopped
2 fresh green chillies, finely chopped
2 teaspoons ground coriander seeds
150 g/5 oz tomatoes, chopped
1 teaspoon garam masala
1 tablespoon finely chopped fresh coriander leaves, to garnish

wash the grams and soak in the measured water overnight. Add the salt and simmer until tender. Drain, reserving the water and set aside.

heat the ghee or oil in a pan, add the onion and fry until golden. Add the cinnamon and cloves and fry for a few seconds, then add the garlic, ginger, chillies and ground coriander and fry for 5 minutes. Add the tomatoes and fry until most of the liquid has evaporated.

add the grams and cook gently for 5 minutes, then add the reserved water and simmer for 20–25 minutes. Add the garam masala and stir well. Sprinkle with the chopped coriander and serve immediately.

Serves 4
Preparation time: *30 minutes*, plus
  overnight soaking time
Cooking time: *45–50 minutes*

clipboard: Grams are chick peas or lentils. When ground, they are used to make gram flour, a common ingredient in Indian cookery.

Vegetable Curry

No Indian meal is complete without a vegetable curry. This one combines aubergines, peas, potatoes and tomatoes, lightly spiced with fennel seeds, chilli powder, coriander seeds and fresh green chillies. Simply scrumptious!

3 tablespoons oil

1 teaspoon fennel seeds

2 onions, sliced

1 teaspoon chilli powder

1 tablespoon ground coriander seeds

2.5 cm/1 inch piece of fresh root ginger, chopped

2 aubergines, sliced

175 g/6 oz shelled peas

125 g/4 oz potatoes, cubed

1 x 250 g/8 oz can tomatoes

4 green chillies, sliced

salt

heat the oil in a large pan, add the fennel seeds and fry for a few seconds, then add the onions and fry until soft and golden. Add the chilli powder, coriander, ginger and salt to taste. Fry for 2 minutes, stirring. Add the aubergines, peas and potatoes and cook for 5 minutes, stirring occasionally.

add the tomatoes along with their juice and the chillies to the pan, cover and simmer for 30 minutes, or until the peas and potatoes are tender and the sauce is thick.

Serves 4
Preparation time: *20 minutes*
Cooking time: *30 minutes*

Balti Mixed Vegetables

Use whichever vegetables are in season, finely diced so that they do not take too long to become tender. The flavours are a subtle blend of ginger, chilli, coriander and turmeric.

2–3 tablespoons vegetable oil
I small onion, chopped
I garlic clove, crushed
2.5 cm/I inch piece of fresh root ginger, grated
I teaspoon chilli powder
2 teaspoons ground coriander
½ teaspoon ground turmeric
500 g/I lb diced mixed vegetables (e.g. potatoes, carrots, swede, peas, beans, cauliflower)
2–3 tomatoes, skinned and chopped, or
4 tablespoons lemon juice
salt

heat the oil in a large wok or heavy-based saucepan and gently fry the onion for 5–10 minutes or until lightly browned. Add the garlic, ginger, chilli powder, coriander, turmeric and a pinch of salt. Fry for 2–3 minutes, add the diced vegetables and stir-fry for a further 2–3 minutes.

add either the chopped tomatoes or the lemon juice. Stir well and add a little water.

cover and cook gently for 10–12 minutes, or until the vegetables are tender, adding a little more water, if necessary, to prevent the vegetables sticking to the bottom of the wok.

serve at once with chapatis or naan (see pages 200 and 202).

Serves 4
Preparation time: *15 minutes*
Cooking time: *20–30 minutes*

Rice and Lentils

Saffron Rice

The combination of rice with saffron threads was made in heaven! This is not the simplest way of cooking rice, but is well worth the effort.

½ teaspoon saffron threads
750 ml/1¼ pints boiling water
175 g/6 oz ghee or 3 tablespoons vegetable oil
2 large onions, sliced
375 g/12 oz Basmati or Patna rice
1 teaspoon cloves
4 cardamoms
1 teaspoon salt
1 teaspoon freshly ground black pepper
silver leaf (varq), to garnish (optional)

put the saffron threads in a small bowl with 1 tablespoon boiling water and leave to soak for 30 minutes. Heat the ghee or vegetable oil in a large heavy-based saucepan, then add the onions. Fry gently for 4–5 minutes until soft.

wash the Basmati or Patna rice thoroughly in a sieve under cold running water and drain well.

add the rice to the onions in the pan and then stir in the cloves, cardamoms, salt and pepper. Fry for 3 minutes, stirring frequently.

pour the remaining boiling water into the pan, together with the saffron and its soaking liquid, then lower the heat and simmer for 15–20 minutes until the rice is cooked.

drain well and transfer the rice to a serving dish. Serve hot, garnished, if liked, with silver leaf.

Serves 4
Preparation time: *15 minutes*, plus
30 minutes soaking time
Cooking time: *30–35 minutes*

clipboard: Varq is edible silver leaf, used for decorative purposes. It is very fragile and should therefore be handled with care. It is available from specialist Indian food stores, though you may have to order it.

Rice with Vegetables

250 g/8 oz frozen diced mixed vegetables

125 g/4 oz frozen diced red and green peppers

125 g/4 oz courgettes, trimmed and sliced

2 tablespoons ground cumin

2 tablespoons ground coriander

1 tablespoon chilli powder

2 teaspoons turmeric

4 teaspoons black peppercorns, crushed

2 teaspoons salt

125 g/4 oz ghee or 2 tablespoons vegetable oil

4 large onions, thinly sliced

5 garlic cloves, thinly sliced

2 x 7 cm/3 inch pieces of fresh root ginger, peeled and sliced

2 x 7 cm/3 inch pieces of cinnamon stick

20 cardamoms

20 cloves

1 tablespoon lovage seeds (optional)

750 g/1½ lb Basmati rice, washed and drained

2 litres/3½ pints boiling water

75 g/3 oz sultanas, to serve

50 g/2 oz flaked almonds, to serve

mix the frozen vegetables with the courgettes and set aside to defrost. Mix together the ground spices and salt. Heat half of the ghee or vegetable oil in a large saucepan, add half of the spice mixture and fry gently for 2 minutes. Stir in the vegetables to coat with the spices and then remove and keep warm.

heat the remaining ghee or vegetable oil in the saucepan and add the onions, garlic and ginger. Fry gently for 5 minutes until soft. Add the pieces of cinnamon stick, cardamoms, cloves and lovage seeds, if using, and fry for 3–4 minutes. Add the remaining spice mixture and fry for 2 minutes.

add the Basmati rice to the saucepan and stir well until all the grains are coated with the spices. Pour in the boiling water and boil gently, uncovered, until the rice is cooked but still firm. Stir occasionally to prevent the rice sticking, adding more boiling water, if necessary.

drain the rice, when ready, into a large sieve. Mix with the reserved vegetables and serve scattered with sultanas and almonds.

Serves 6–8
Preparation time: *15 minutes*
Cooking time: *35–40 minutes*

Spices

Saffron

Coriander seeds

Cardamom pods

Dried red chilli

Cardamom pods
The cardamom pod is a small, pale green, oval-shaped pod, which protects some small black seeds. Cardamom is a member of the ginger family. It is a highly aromatic spice and is essential to Indian cuisine. The pods are picked before they are ripe and, once they are dried, they can be ground or used whole. Cardamom is one of the main ingredients in curry powder. It is also used in pickles and rice dishes, and is very good in certain sweet dishes. It should be used sparingly as it is an expensive spice, as each pod has to be hand picked. Cardamom seeds are often chewed after a meal as a breath freshener.

Saffron threads
These are made from the dried, thread-like stamens of the saffron crocus. The stamens are a dark orange colour and are highly fragrant. Saffron is the most expensive and most highly prized spice on the market, as each crocus has three stamens and each one must be hand picked. Saffron threads are used in fish dishes, rice and many other Asian and Indian dishes. They are also used in some sweet recipes, such as ice-cream and cookies. In order to use saffron, the strands can be either soaked in hot milk, water or stock for 15 minutes before being added to a dish, or they can be roasted in a metal spoon directly over a low heat until they are crisp enough to be crushed.

Coriander seeds
The small oval coriander seeds have a particularly fine lemony flavour. They can be used whole, ground or roasted. Coriander seeds are a very important ingredient in curry powder, and they can also be used in pickles, chutney and marinades.

Dried red chillies
Tiny red peppers with a fiercely fiery heat, chillies were first grown in the Amazon region of South America and in Mexico. Their arrival in India, where they were exported to the trading posts, was to revolutionize Indian cooking. Dried chillies are easy to use: simply cut off the stems, shake out the seeds, and then break the pepper into little pieces and cover these with hot water.

Cinnamon

Cumin seeds

Chilli powder

Turmeric

Leave for 15–20 minutes and then drain, reserving the water. Chop the chillies roughly and put them in a small blender or electric mill with half the soaking water and process to a purée. Chillies must be used with caution, as they are profoundly hot and can even damage the mucus membrane inside the mouth, nose, throat, stomach and intestine if used in too large quantities. The best remedy for a burning sensation after eating chillies is cold dairy food such as yogurt, milk or ice-cream. If they are stored properly, chillies will keep forever and maintain both their attractive red colour and their fiery taste.

Turmeric
This is a spice taken from the dried roots of a tropical plant related to the ginger family. Turmeric is ground to produce a bright yellow powder. It has a mild bittersweet flavour and is used in pickles, chutneys and mustard. In Thailand, the roots are boiled and used as a vegetable, but in Indian cuisine it is mainly used as a colouring agent to impart a strong yellow to foods, particularly rice dishes.

Cinnamon
Cinnamon is a popular bark-like spice, which is light brown in colour and has a strong, sweet aroma. It comes from an evergreen tree in Sri Lanka, and is often used in soups, baking, liqueurs and oils.

Chilli powder
This is the combination of ground, dried chilli peppers and other seasonings. It is a dark red powder with a spicy, peppery taste. It is used to flavour many chilli dishes, one of the most popular being Chilli Con Carne. It should be used sparingly because of its strong flavour. When buying chilli powder, purchase small amounts as it has a limited shelf life and rapidly loses its flavour.

Cumin seeds
The seeds of the cumin plant are long and pale brown. They are very aromatic with a pungent flavour. Cumin seeds are one of the most important spices in Indian cuisine, and are used in most dishes. The seeds can be roasted to bring out their flavour.

Kitcheree

Basmati rice is cooked with yellow lentils and gently spiced with cloves, cardamom seeds, a piece of cinnamon stick, and turmeric.

250 g/8 oz Basmati rice
250 g/8 oz yellow lentils (moong dhal)
75 g/3 oz ghee or 1½ tablespoons vegetable oil
1 garlic clove, sliced
5 cloves
5 cardamom seeds
5 cm/2 inch piece of cinnamon stick
1 small onion, sliced
1 teaspoon turmeric
½ teaspoon salt

To garnish
fried onion rings
chopped fresh coriander leaves

mix the rice and lentils together and then wash thoroughly in cold running water. Drain well, place in a bowl and cover with cold water and leave to soak for 1 hour.

heat the ghee or vegetable oil in a large pan and fry the garlic, cloves, cardamom seeds and cinnamon for 1 minute. Add the onion and fry for 1–2 minutes.

drain the rice and lentils thoroughly and then add them to the onion and spices in the pan. Stir in the turmeric and salt, and toss gently over a low heat for 5 minutes.

add enough boiling water to cover the rice by 2.5 cm/1 inch, and then cover the pan with a tightly fitting lid. Simmer over a low heat for 30–45 minutes until the rice is cooked and the liquid absorbed. Serve garnished with fried onion rings and chopped coriander.

Serves 4
Preparation time: *15 minutes*, plus
1 hour soaking time
Cooking time: *40–55 minutes*

Vegetable Biriyani

Vegetables and rice are cooked together to make a glorious one-pot meal. A mixture of curd cheese, sultanas and chopped nuts, including almonds, cashews and pistachios, is the perfect finishing touch.

3 tablespoons ghee or vegetable oil

1 large onion, finely chopped

2 garlic cloves, chopped

8 cloves

2 x 2.5 cm/1 inch pieces of cinnamon stick

4 green cardamoms

1 teaspoon turmeric

1 teaspoon garam masala

500 g/1 lb Basmati rice, pre-soaked

250 g/8 oz mixed diced vegetables (e.g. carrots, cauliflower, courgettes, okra, peas)

600 ml/1 pint Vegetable Stock (see page 11)

50 g/2 oz panir (curd cheese), lightly fried

50 g/2 oz sultanas

125 g/4 oz chopped mixed nuts (e.g. almonds, cashew nuts, pistachios)

salt

heat the ghee or vegetable oil in a large saucepan and fry the onion until golden. Remove half of the fried onion and set aside for the garnish. Add the garlic and spices to the pan and fry for 2–3 minutes.

rinse the Basmati rice in cold running water and then drain well. Add to the pan and stir well. Cook for a further 5 minutes until all the grains are glistening and translucent.

add the mixed diced vegetables and salt to taste, together with the stock, and bring to the boil. Cover the pan and reduce the heat to a bare simmer. Cook gently for 20–25 minutes until all the liquid has been absorbed and the rice is cooked.

stir in the panir, sultanas and nuts and mix well. Cover and cook for 5 minutes over a low heat until all the moisture has evaporated. Serve hot, sprinkled with the reserved fried onion.

Serves 4–6
Preparation time: *15 minutes*
Cooking time: *40–45 minutes*

Masoor Dhal

This spicy lentil dish, flavoured with onion, garlic and lemon juice, is high in nutrients as well as tasting delicious, so you can feel smug about its benefits as well as enjoying its fantastic flavours.

4 tablespoons oil
6 cloves
6 cardamoms
2.5 cm/1 inch piece of cinnamon stick
1 onion, chopped
2.5 cm/1 inch piece of fresh root ginger, chopped
1 fresh green chilli, finely chopped
1 garlic clove, chopped
½ teaspoon garam masala
250 g/8 oz lentils
4 tablespoons lemon juice
salt
2–3 dried chillies, to garnish (optional)

heat the oil in a pan, add the cloves, cardamoms and cinnamon and fry until they start to swell.

add the onion and fry until translucent. Add the ginger, chilli, garlic and garam masala and cook for about 5 minutes.

add the lentils, stir thoroughly and fry for 1 minute. Add salt to taste and enough water to come about 3 cm/1¼ inches above the level of the lentils. Bring to the boil, cover and simmer for about 20 minutes, until really thick and tender.

sprinkle with the lemon juice, stir and serve immediately, garnished with dried chillies, if liked.

Serves 4
Preparation time: *20 minutes*
Cooking time: *25 minutes*

clipboard: Lentils are full of nutrients and have a high energy value. They are rich in protein, carbohydrates, phosphorus and iron, as well as the B vitamins.

Prawn and Spinach Rice

500 g/1 lb Basmati rice
2 teaspoons salt
½ teaspoon turmeric
50 g/2 oz butter
3 tablespoons oil
2 onions sliced
3 garlic cloves, finely chopped
1 tablespoon grated fresh root ginger
1–2 teaspoons chilli powder
2 teaspoons ground coriander
1 kg/2 lb spinach, washed, trimmed and chopped
500 g/1 lb cooked peeled prawns

place the Basmati rice in a sieve and wash it thoroughly under cold running water. Drain well. Fill a large saucepan two-thirds full with water and bring to the boil. Add the rice to the saucepan together with 1 teaspoon of the salt and the turmeric. Boil for 3 minutes and then drain. Stir in the butter.

heat the oil in a large saucepan and add the onions, garlic and ginger. Fry for 5 minutes until golden. Stir in the chilli powder, coriander and the remaining 1 teaspoon of salt, and fry for a few seconds.

add the spinach and cook, stirring constantly, until softened. Stir in the prawns and then remove from the heat.

layer the spinach mixture with the buttered rice in an ovenproof casserole dish, beginning and ending with the spinach. Cover tightly and cook in a preheated oven at 180°C/350°F/Gas Mark 4 for 30 minutes. Serve immediately.

Serves 4
Preparation time: *30 minutes*
Cooking time: *30 minutes*
Oven temperature:
    180°C/350°F/Gas Mark 4

Pilau Rice

with sultanas and nuts

2 tablespoons ghee or vegetable oil

6 cardamoms, bruised

5 whole cloves

7 cm/3 inch piece of cinnamon stick, broken in half

½ teaspoon black peppercorns, lightly crushed

¼ teaspoon saffron threads

375 g/12 oz Basmati rice

¾ teaspoon salt

½ teaspoon orange flower water (optional)

600 ml/1 pint water

25 g/1 oz sultanas

25 g/1 oz roasted cashew nuts

25 g/1 oz pistachio nuts

heat the ghee or vegetable oil in a wide heavy-based saucepan. Stir in the cardamoms, cloves, cinnamon stick and peppercorns and fry over a gentle heat, stirring constantly, for 2 minutes until fragrant. Add the saffron threads and Basmati rice to the pan and fry, stirring constantly, for a further minute.

add the salt, orange flower water, if using, and measured water. Stir well to mix. Bring to the boil, then reduce the heat, cover the pan and cook the rice gently for 15 minutes without removing the lid.

remove the pan from the heat and lightly loosen the rice grains with a fork. (All the water should have been absorbed.) Stir the sultanas into the rice, cover the pan with a clean dry tea towel and allow the rice to cook in its own heat for a further 5 minutes.

stir both the cashew nuts and pistachios into the rice just before serving. Serve hot.

Serves 4–6
Preparation time: *5 minutes*
Cooking time: *25 minutes*

clipboard: Orange flower water is a delicate flavouring which, although not essential, enhances the subtle flavour of the rice. It is available from the baking counter of most supermarkets.

Breads and
Accompaniments

Puri Stuffed with Dhal

175 g/6 oz dried black beans
500 g/1 lb plain flour
1 fresh green chilli, chopped
½ teaspoon salt
vegetable oil for deep-frying
fresh coriander leaves, to garnish

Spices

1 tablespoon aniseed
1 teaspoon coriander seeds
½ teaspoon white cumin seeds
½ teaspoon red chilli powder
¼ teaspoon asafoetida powder

soak the black beans in water overnight. Rinse them in cold running water and drain well. Sift the flour into a bowl and gradually add enough cold water to make a soft dough. Cover this with a damp cloth and then set aside for 30 minutes.

grind the drained beans with the chilli, salt and all the spices to make the stuffing. You can do this in an electric grinder or food processor if wished. Mix well.

divide the dough into 16 portions, using wet hands, and smear each one with a little of the vegetable oil. Flatten each piece of dough and roll out to a 5 cm/2 inch diameter circle.

wrap a portion of the stuffing in each circle of dough and, with greased hands, roll into smooth balls. Flatten each ball with a rolling pin into a 7 cm/3 inch round. Heat the oil for deep-frying and fry the puri one at a time until golden on both sides. Drain on absorbent kitchen paper and serve garnished with coriander.

Makes 16
Preparation time: *30 minutes*, plus overnight
  soaking time, plus 30 minutes standing time
Cooking time: *20 minutes*

clipboard: Black beans are salted, fermented beans with a salty flavour. They are sold in packs or by weight, and must be soaked for 5–10 minutes before use.

Chapatis

250 g/8 oz wholemeal flour
1 teaspoon salt
200 ml/7 fl oz water
ghee or vegetable oil for greasing
butter, to serve

place the flour and salt in a bowl and make a well in the centre. Gradually stir in the water, a little at a time, and mix to form a soft, supple dough.

knead the dough on a lightly floured surface for 10 minutes, and then cover the dough and leave in a cool place for 30 minutes. Knead again thoroughly and then divide the dough into 12 equal-sized pieces.

roll out each piece of dough, using a rolling pin on a lightly floured surface, until they form thin round 'pancakes'.

grease a griddle or heavy-based frying pan lightly with a little ghee or vegetable oil and place over a moderate heat. Add a chapati to the pan and cook until blisters appear. Press down firmly with a fish slice and then turn it over and cook the other side until lightly coloured. Remove and keep warm while you cook the other chapatis.

serve brushed with a little butter and folded into quarters.

Makes 12
Preparation time: *15 minutes*, plus
  30 minutes standing time
Cooking time: *12 minutes*

Naan

Naan is a delicious, puffy Indian bread, made with milk and yogurt, which is just the thing for mopping up spicy curries and baltis. This one is spread with butter and poppy seeds before cooking under a preheated grill.

375 g/12 oz plain flour
1½ teaspoons sugar
1 teaspoon salt
½ teaspoon baking powder
15 g/½ oz fresh yeast
150 ml/¼ pint warm milk
150 ml/¼ pint natural yogurt
ghee or vegetable oil for greasing
125 g/4 oz butter
2 tablespoons poppy seeds

sift the flour into a large bowl and stir in the sugar, salt and baking powder. Dissolve the yeast in the milk and stir in the yogurt. Mix thoroughly with the flour to form a dough.

knead the dough until it is smooth, and then place in a bowl covered with a clean cloth and leave it to rise in a warm place for about 4 hours.

divide the risen dough into 12 equal-sized portions and roll them into balls. On a lightly floured surface, flatten the balls into oblong shapes, using both hands and slapping the naan from one hand to the other.

grease a griddle or heavy-based frying pan lightly with ghee or vegetable oil and heat it until it is very hot. Cook the naan on one side only, a few at a time. Remove and spread the raw side with butter and poppy seeds. Cook under a preheated hot grill until browned. Serve hot.

Makes 12
Preparation time: *30 minutes*, plus
  4 hours proving time
Cooking time: *30 minutes*

Paratha

Paratha is a wholemeal dough, lightly brushed with a little oil or ghee and cooked on a griddle or a heavy-based frying pan. It tastes marvellous with spicy foods.

250 g/8 oz wholemeal flour
I teaspoon salt
200 ml/7 fl oz water (approximately)
50–75 g/2–3 oz melted ghee or 1–1½ tablespoons vegetable oil

place the flour and salt in a bowl. Make a well in the centre, gradually stir in the water and work to a soft supple dough. Knead for 10 minutes, then cover and leave in a cool place for 30 minutes. Knead again very thoroughly, then divide into 6 pieces.

roll out each piece on a floured surface into a thin circle. Brush with melted ghee or vegetable oil and fold in half; brush again and fold in half again. Roll out again to a circle about 3 mm/⅛ inch thick.

grease a griddle or heavy-based frying pan lightly with a little ghee or vegetable oil and place over a moderate heat. Add a paratha and cook for 1 minute. Lightly brush the top with a little ghee or vegetable oil and turn over. Brush all round the edge with ghee or vegetable oil and cook until golden. Remove from the pan and keep warm while cooking the rest. Serve hot.

Makes 6
Preparation time: *35 minutes*, plus 30
  minutes standing time
Cooking time: *15 minutes*

Puri

Puris are deep-fried wholemeal pancakes, popular in some parts of India. Serve them to accompany spicy sauces and curries, or just as a little snack.

250 g/8 oz wholemeal flour, or half wholemeal and half plain white flour
¼ teaspoon salt
150 ml/¼ pint warm water (approximately)
2 teaspoons melted ghee or vegetable oil
oil for deep-frying

place the wholemeal flour and salt in a bowl; sift in the plain flour, if using. Make a well in the centre, add the measured water gradually and work to a dough. Knead in the ghee or vegetable oil, then knead for 10 minutes until smooth and elastic. Cover and set aside for 30 minutes.

divide the dough into 16 pieces. With lightly oiled hands, pat each piece into a ball. Lightly oil the pastry board and rolling pin and roll out each ball into a thin circular 'pancake'.

heat the oil and deep-fry the puris very quickly, turning them over once, until deep golden in colour. Drain well and serve immediately.

Makes 16
Preparation time: *30 minutes*, plus
 30 minutes standing time
Cooking time: *20–30 minutes*

Raita

As popular as chutney, this is a classic Indian accompaniment, consisting of yogurt and cucumber, which helps take some of the heat out of the spicy dishes with which you serve it.

100 g/3½ oz cucumber, thinly sliced, plus extra to garnish
2 x 150 g/5 oz cartons natural yogurt
50 g/2 oz spring onions, thinly sliced
1 fresh green chilli, deseeded and finely chopped
coriander leaves, to garnish
salt

place the cucumber in a colander, sprinkle with salt and leave to drain for 30 minutes. Dry thoroughly.

mix the yogurt with salt to taste and fold in the cucumber, spring onion and chilli. Arrange in a serving dish, garnish with some extra slices of cucumber and chill until required.

Serves 4
Preparation time: *5 minutes*, plus 30 minutes standing time

clipboard: Raita can also be made using other vegetables as well as cucumber, and with fruit. Banana, for example, makes a particularly good raita.

Cachumber
with onion and tomatoes

This quickly prepared accompaniment is an Indian version of the ever popular tomato salsa. It is delicious as a dip, but also proves an ideal partner to vegetable curries.

1 onion, chopped
250 g/8 oz tomatoes, skinned and chopped
1–2 fresh green chillies, chopped
1–2 tablespoons vinegar
salt

put the onion, tomatoes and chillies in a dish. Pour over the vinegar (the mixture must not be too liquid) and salt to taste. Chill before serving.

Serves 4
Preparation time: *5 minutes*

clipboard: A red onion is probably the best variety to use for this spicy onion and tomato dish. Red onions are not so strong as others and are slightly sweet.

Breads

Poppadum

Naan

Parathas

Poppadum
Poppadums are flat, crisp breads with a particularly crunchy texture. They are available either plain or spiced, and in different sizes. They can be served to accompany main meals, or as a starter with a sauce or chutneys. They are widely available in packets in many supermarkets.

Parathas
Breads play a very important part in the Indian diet, and parathas are cooked almost on a daily basis in the great majority of Indian households. The paratha is a popular flat bread made with wholemeal flour. Parathas can also be stuffed with various fillings. In Indian cafés, parathas are deep-fried and served with freshly barbecued kebabs.

Naan
Naan bread is the exception to most Indian breads in that it is unleavened. It is often used as an accompaniment to curries and baltis – almost as an eating utensil to mop up sauces or pieces of food. Naan are cooked in a tandoor oven, which is heated to a fierce temperature. They are made with yeast and are delicious served hot. Naan can also be flavoured with garlic or herbs. The peshawari naan – which comes from Peshawar in Pakistan and is becoming increasingly popular in the West – is stuffed with almonds and is slightly sweet. When it is eaten with a curry, it adds an interesting sweet and sour flavour. Keema naan is stuffed with a filling made of minced meat.

Chapatis

Mini Poppadums

Mini Naan

Chapatis

The chapati is one of the less fattening Indian breads, as it does not contain any fat – though some people in India like to brush it with a little melted butter made from buffaloes' milk, just before serving. It is a flat circular Indian bread, a little like a pancake, made with wholemeal flour. It should be eaten hot, straight from the pan, when it will be swollen and crisp. If it is not practical to serve it straight away, it can be kept warm by wrapping it in aluminium foil. In India, chapatis are cooked over a naked flame so that the bread puffs up. It can also be cooked on a griddle. Chapatis may be filled with chopped spinach flavoured with ginger and cumin, in which case they will not be quite as crisp.

Mini Poppadums

Mini-poppadums are now sold in packets in many supermarkets. They are delicious eaten as a snack between meals, or they can be served with chutneys and dips either as a starter or as an accompaniment to a main meal.

Mini Naan

Naan breads come in all sorts of shapes and sizes nowadays to suit the particular occasion. Mini-naan are ideal to serve as quick snacks, or they can be served as a starter.

Mango Chutney

Home-made mango chutney is far superior to the commercially prepared varieties. Use firm mangoes, which are just ripe but not yet soft. This chutney will keep for several months in an air-tight jar.

500 g/I lb sugar
600 ml/I pint vinegar
5 cm/2 inch piece of fresh root ginger
4 garlic cloves
I kg/2 lb very firm mangoes, peeled and cut into small pieces
½–I tablespoon chilli powder
I tablespoon mustard seeds
2 tablespoons salt
125 g/4 oz raisins or sultanas

place the sugar and all but 1 tablespoon of the vinegar in a saucepan and simmer for 10 minutes.

work the ginger, garlic and remaining vinegar to a paste in a blender or food processor. Add to the pan and cook for 10 minutes, stirring.

add the mango and remaining ingredients to the pan and cook, uncovered, for about 25 minutes, stirring as the chutney thickens. Remove from the heat and allow to cool.

pour into hot sterilized jars, making sure that the lid is air-tight.

Makes about 1.25 kg/2½ lb
Preparation time: *35 minutes*
Cooking time: *25 minutes*

Prawn Relish

This aromatic relish, in which prawns are spiced with red and green chillies, cumin seeds, turmeric, ginger and curry leaves, makes a delicious accompaniment to Indian food.

2 tablespoons oil
I onion, chopped
4 dried red chillies
2 fresh green chillies, chopped
½ teaspoon cumin seeds
½ teaspoon turmeric
I garlic clove, crushed
2.5 cm/I inch piece of fresh root ginger, chopped
4 curry leaves, crumbled
150 g/5 oz prawns
I tablespoon vinegar
salt

heat the oil in a pan, add the onion and fry until golden. Crumble in the dried chillies. Add the fresh chillies, cumin seeds, turmeric, garlic, ginger and curry leaves and fry for 2 minutes. Add the prawns and fry for 2 minutes.

add the vinegar and season with salt to taste. Simmer, uncovered, for 3–4 minutes, until most of the liquid has evaporated. Serve hot or cold.

Serves 4
Preparation time: *5 minutes*
Cooking time: *20 minutes*

clipboard: Curry leaves are the aromatic leaves of the sweet Nim tree and are available dried. They release a spicy, appetizing smell when they are cooked.

Date and Tomato Chutney

This chutney, which is made with dates, tomatoes and onions, makes a welcome alternative to the other chutneys that are more usually served with Indian food, such as mango chutney or lime pickle.

250 g/8 oz dates, pitted and chopped
1 x 575 g/1 lb 3 oz can tomatoes
1 onion, chopped
3.5 cm/1½ inch piece of fresh root ginger, chopped
1 teaspoon chilli powder
1 teaspoon salt
6 tablespoons vinegar

put all the ingredients in a saucepan and stir well. Bring to the boil, then simmer, uncovered, for about 45 minutes, stirring occasionally until thick. Serve cold.

note that extra chilli powder and salt may be added if wished, according to taste.

Serves 4–6
Preparation time: *10 minutes*
Cooking time: *45 minutes*

Ginger Chutney

Another unusual chutney, this one is made with fresh root ginger, puréed with lemon juice, sugar, sultanas and garlic. It does not keep but needs to be eaten fresh.

8 tablespoons lemon juice
25 g/1 oz sugar
140 g/4 ½ oz fresh root ginger, finely chopped
75 g/3 oz sultanas
1 garlic clove, crushed
salt

place all the ingredients in a blender or food processor and work to a smooth purée.

transfer the mixture to a small serving dish and chill until ready to serve. Eat within 2 days.

Makes about 300 ml/½ pint
Preparation time: *5 minutes*

clipboard: Sultanas come from grapes that are green when fresh but darken in colour when they are dried. In general, lighter-coloured sultanas are obtained by being dried in the shade, while darker sultanas are obtained by being dried in the sun.

Brinjal Pickle

This pickle is for those who like hot relishes, but the quantity of chillies can be reduced if you prefer a milder taste.

1 kg/2 lb aubergines, thinly sliced
1 tablespoon salt
300 ml/½ pint hot water
125 g/4 oz tamarind
50 g/2 oz cumin seeds
25 g/1 oz dried red chillies
50 g/2 oz fresh root ginger, chopped
50 g/2 oz garlic
300 ml/½ pint vinegar
150 ml/¼ pint oil
2 teaspoons mustard seeds
250 g/8 oz sugar

sprinkle the aubergines with the salt and leave in a colander for 30 minutes to drain. Pour the hot water on to the tamarind and leave to soak for 20 minutes. Press through a fine sieve and set aside.

put the cumin, chillies, ginger, garlic and 2 tablespoons of the vinegar into a blender or food processor and work to a paste.

heat the oil in a large saucepan and fry the mustard seeds until they begin to splutter. Quickly add the spice paste and fry, stirring, for 2 minutes. Add the aubergine, tamarind water, remaining vinegar and the sugar and stir well. Bring to the boil, then simmer for 30–35 minutes until the mixture is thick and pulpy.

leave until cold, then pour into sterilized jars and cover with a wax disc and screw-top lid. Store in a cool place.

Makes about 1.5 kg/3 lb
Preparation time: *5 minutes*, plus
30 minutes standing time
Cooking time: *40–45 minutes*

Sambal Bajak

A pungent pickle, this is made using onions, garlic, shrimp paste, fresh red chillies and lime juice. It has a fiery kick, and is not for the faint-hearted!

2 tablespoons oil
3 small onions, finely chopped
4 garlic cloves, finely chopped
I teaspoon blachan or shrimp paste
125 g/4 oz fresh red chillies, chopped
4 tablespoons lime juice
I teaspoon salt
I teaspoon brown sugar

heat the oil in a small frying pan, add the onions and garlic and fry until golden brown. Add the blachan or shrimp paste and fry, stirring and mashing, for 1 minute.

stir in the remaining ingredients and fry, stirring, for 5 minutes or until the mixture is fairly dry.

allow to cool, then spoon into a jar. Cover and keep refrigerated until required.

Serves 4
Preparation time: *5 minutes*
Cooking time: *15 minutes*

clipboard: Blachan is a strong-smelling, salty shrimp paste, available in cans or packets from specialist food stores. It has a very pungent smell, so you should keep it tightly sealed in the refrigerator once it has been opened. It should always be well fried, or wrapped in foil and roasted, before it is used.

Brinjal Sambal

This aubergine pickle is not overly spicy, largely because of the addition of coconut milk. It makes a good accompaniment to spicy meat or vegetable dishes.

1 large aubergine
1 small onion, finely chopped
3 fresh green chillies, finely chopped
1 cm/½ inch piece of fresh root ginger, cut into fine strips
2 tablespoons thick coconut milk
½ teaspoon salt
4 tablespoons lemon juice

place the aubergine on a baking sheet and cook in a preheated moderate oven, 180°C/350°F/Gas Mark 4, for 30 minutes or until soft. Leave to cool slightly, then slit it open and scoop out the flesh into a bowl.

mash the aubergine with a fork and mix in the remaining ingredients. Taste the Sambal and adjust the seasoning. Serve chilled.

Serves 4
Preparation time: *10 minutes*, plus chilling time
Cooking time: *30 minutes*
Oven temperature: 180°C/350°F/Gas Mark 4

Sambal Oelek
with chillies and lemon juice

125 g/4 oz fresh red chillies, chopped
2 tablespoons lemon or lime juice, or vinegar
1 teaspoon sugar
1 teaspoon salt

put all the ingredients into a blender or food processor and work until the chillies are finely chopped. Adjust the seasoning, to taste. Spoon into a jar, cover with a screw-top lid and keep refrigerated until required.

Serves 4
Preparation time: *5 minutes*

Desserts

Batter Coils in Syrup

175 g/6 oz plain flour
50 g/2 oz gram flour (besan), lightly dry-fried
4 tablespoons natural yogurt
5 g/¼ oz fresh yeast
vegetable oil, for deep-frying

Syrup
300 ml/½ pint water
250 g/8 oz sugar
½ teaspoon ground saffron
½ teaspoon green cardamom seeds, ground

place the plain and gram flours in a large bowl and mix in the yogurt, yeast and enough water to make a thick creamy batter. Set aside for about 2 hours to ferment.

put the water and sugar in a saucepan and stir over a low heat until all the sugar has dissolved. Bring to the boil, still stirring, and cook until the syrup has reached the thread stage, 110°C/225°F. Just before the syrup is ready, add the ground saffron and ground cardamom seeds.

heat the vegetable oil in a pan until a cube of day-old bread dropped in turns golden in 1 minute. Whisk the batter thoroughly and then pour in a steady stream through a perforated spoon to form coils in the pan below. Make a few coils at a time and deep-fry for about 30 seconds turning them so that they are golden and crisp all over.

remove the coils from the pan and drain on absorbent kitchen paper. Immerse them in the prepared syrup for 3–4 minutes to soak up as much syrup as possible. Remove and serve immediately while they are hot and crisp.

Serves 4–6
Preparation time: *15 minutes*, plus
  2 hours standing time
Cooking time: *20 minutes*

Coconut Pudding

There is nothing quite like the flavour of fresh coconut. The preparation for this dish is a little complicated, but it's well worth the effort.

2 fresh coconuts
450 ml/¾ pint boiling water
250 g/8 oz caster sugar
175 g/6 oz rice flour
2 eggs, beaten
50 g/2 oz slivered almonds
shredded coconut, to decorate

make some holes in the eyes of the coconuts and then carefully drain out the liquid over a bowl and reserve for later.

crack open the coconuts and separate the flesh from the shells. Grate the flesh into a bowl and then pour the boiling water over it. Leave to stand for 15 minutes and then strain the liquid through a sieve lined with double muslin, held over a bowl.

gather up the muslin and squeeze out as much coconut milk as possible. Discard the coconut in the cloth. Mix the strained coconut milk with the liquid extracted from the coconuts and then beat in all the remaining ingredients.

pour the mixture into a large heavy-based saucepan and bring to the boil. Reduce the heat and simmer until the liquid thickens, stirring constantly. Pour into a greased 20 cm/8 inch round baking tin and bake in a preheated oven at 180°C/350°F/Gas Mark 4 for 30 minutes, until browned. Serve hot, decorated with coconut.

Serves 4
Preparation time: *35 minutes*, plus
  standing time
Cooking time: *30 minutes*
Oven temperature:
  180°C/350°F/Gas Mark 4

Mango Ice Cream

425 g/14 oz canned mango pulp
3 tablespoons clear honey
600 ml/1 pint double cream
50 g/2 oz ground almonds
4 egg whites
mint leaves, to decorate

warm the mango pulp in a saucepan over a gentle heat and then stir in the honey until melted. Remove from the heat and stir in the cream and the ground almonds until they are evenly mixed. Set aside and cool.

pour the mango ice cream mixture into a freezer container and place in the freezer. Freeze for about 4 hours or until the mango mixture is just beginning to freeze around the edges and becoming slushy.

remove the container from the freezer and turn out the mango ice cream into a bowl. Carefully break up the mixture with a fork.

whisk the egg whites in a clean bowl until stiff and then gently fold them into the half-frozen mixture. Return to the freezer container and freeze for a further 4 hours until solid. Remove the ice cream from the freezer about 20 minutes before serving to soften slightly. Decorate with mint leaves.

Serves 8
Preparation time: *20 minutes*
Freezing time: *8 hours*

Deep-Fried Milk Pastries

1 litre/1¾ pints milk
8 tablespoons lemon juice
125 g/4 oz semolina
vegetable oil for deep-frying

Syrup
300 ml/½ pint water
5 cardamoms
5 cloves
250 g/8 oz sugar
2 teaspoons rosewater

heat the milk in a saucepan, add the lemon juice and bring to the boil. Don't worry when the milk curdles. Boil for 5–10 minutes and then leave to cool. Drain off the whey, leaving the curds behind. Tie the curds up in a double thickness of muslin and place in a sieve. Weight down and leave overnight.

mix the resulting cheese (panir) with the semolina on the following day, to form a dough. Break into about 15 equal-sized pieces and roll into smooth balls. Heat the oil for deep-frying until a ball of dough, when dropped into the pan, immediately starts to sizzle and floats to the surface.

deep-fry the balls in batches until evenly golden brown. Remove with a slotted spoon and drain on absorbent kitchen paper. Keep them warm in a low oven while you make the syrup.

bring the water to the boil in a pan with the cardamoms and cloves. Reduce the heat, add the sugar and stir until dissolved. Increase the heat and boil rapidly, without stirring, until the syrup starts to thicken. Cool slightly and add the rosewater. Serve the pastry balls warm in the syrup.

Serves 4–6
Preparation time: *30 minutes*, plus
  overnight standing time
Cooking time: *25 minutes*

Kheer

This Indian variation on rice pudding, delicately flavoured with sultanas and flaked almonds or pistachio nuts, is absolutely wonderful.

75 g/3 oz long-grain rice
1.8 litres/3 pints milk
50 g/2 oz sultanas (optional)
caster sugar to taste
150 ml/¼ pint single cream

To decorate
flaked almonds
rose petals

place the rice and 1 litre/1¾ pints of the milk in a heavy-based pan. Cook gently at simmering point for 45–60 minutes until most of the milk has been absorbed.

add the remaining milk and the sultanas, if using, stir well and continue simmering until thickened. Remove from the heat and add sugar to taste.

leave until completely cold, stirring occasionally to prevent a skin forming, then stir in the cream.

turn into small dishes and serve cold, sprinkled with flaked almonds or pistachio nuts. Decorate with rose petals.

Serves 4
Preparation time: *5 minutes*, plus
   chilling time
Cooking time: *1–1¼ hours*

Almond Barfi

The Indians are good at imaginative milk puddings, and this one is no exception. The milk is slowly cooked until it becomes thick and lumpy, when it is flavoured with almonds and crushed cardamoms.

750 ml/1¼ pints full-cream milk
50 g/2 oz caster sugar
50 g/2 oz ground almonds
6 cardamoms, peeled and crushed

cook the milk in a large heavy-based saucepan for about 1¼ hours, until it is reduced to a thick lumpy consistency. Stir occasionally and be careful not to let the milk burn.

stir in the sugar then add the almonds and cook for 2 minutes. Pour into a buttered tray and sprinkle with the crushed cardamoms. Serve warm, cut into squares.

Serves 4
Preparation time: *5 minutes*
Cooking time: *1¼ hours*

Shrikand

This yogurt-based dessert looks as good as it tastes. Flavoured with saffron and rosewater, it is guaranteed to impress your guests.

I kg/2 lb natural yogurt
¼ teaspoon saffron threads
2 tablespoons caster sugar
I tablespoon rosewater

To decorate
1–2 teaspoons cardamom seeds, crushed
I tablespoon pistachio nuts, shelled and chopped

turn the yogurt into a sieve lined with muslin and leave to drip over a bowl for 6 hours. Put the dried curds – there will be about 300 g/10 oz – into a bowl and beat in the saffron. Add the sugar and taste; add a little more if you like, but it should not be too sweet.

mix in the rosewater, a little at a time, until the mixture resembles thick cream. Cover and chill until required.

spoon into individual bowls and decorate with the cardamoms and pistachio nuts to serve.

Serves 4
Preparation time: *5 minutes*, plus 6 hours
standing time, plus chilling time

clipboard: Rosewater is used to flavour creams, ice-creams and pastries, as well as liqueurs and wines. It is available from the baking section of supermarkets and delicatessens.

Mawa

The ingredients are very simple, the preparation is simpler still, but something magical happens during the cooking time to turn this into a magical Indian-style toffee.

1.8 litres/3 pints full-cream milk
3–4 tablespoons caster sugar
2 leaves varq (silver leaf)
handful edible flowers (e.g. nasturtiums or pansies), to decorate

cook the milk in a large heavy-based saucepan for about 1¼ hours, until it is reduced to a thick, lumpy consistency. Stir occasionally and be careful not to let the milk burn.

add the sugar and continue cooking for 10 minutes.

spread the mixture on a lightly buttered plate: it should be a light cream-coloured, softly set toffee.

cut into wedges and serve cold decorated with strips of varq and edible flower petals.

Serves 4–6
Preparation time: *5 minutes*
Cooking time: *1 hour 25 minutes*

Carrot Halva

Carrots hardly ever feature on the dessert menu, but this recipe is set to change all that and carrots take a well-deserved bow, with the help of a little golden syrup and sultanas.

1.2 litres/2 pints milk
250 g/8 oz carrot, finely grated
75 g/3 oz butter
1 tablespoon golden syrup
125 g/4 oz sugar
50 g/2 oz sultanas or raisins

To decorate
1 teaspoon cardamoms
2 leaves varq (silver leaf)

place the milk and grated carrot in a heavy-based saucepan and cook over a high heat, stirring occasionally, until the liquid has evaporated. Add the butter, syrup, sugar and sultanas or raisins. Stir until the butter and sugar have melted, then cook for 15–20 minutes, stirring frequently, until the mixture starts to leave the side of the pan.

pour into a shallow buttered dish and spread evenly. Decorate with cardamoms and strips of varq. Cut into slices and serve warm or cold.

Serves 4–6
Preparation time: *5 minutes*
Cooking time: *45–50 minutes*

Kulfi

Blanched almonds combine with milk, double cream and rosewater to produce this unusual and impressive ice-cream. Garnished with rose petals, it looks marvellous.

250 g/8 oz blanched almonds
1.8 litres/3 pints milk
250 g/8 oz caster sugar
300 ml/½ pint double cream
2 tablespoons rosewater

place the almonds in a bowl, cover with cold water and set aside. Reserve 300 ml/½ pint of the milk and bring the rest to the boil in a large heavy-based or non-stick saucepan. Simmer until the milk is reduced by half, stirring from time to time to ensure that any skin or solids that cling to the side of the pan are well mixed in.

drain the almonds and place three-quarters of them in a blender or food processor with the reserved milk. Blend the mixture for a few seconds until the almonds are roughly ground; the mixture should be crunchy. Add the almond mixture and sugar to the hot milk and continue simmering for a further 10–20 minutes, stirring constantly. Remove the pan from the heat and leave to cool to room temperature, then place in the refrigerator until well chilled.

chop the remaining almonds roughly and add them to the chilled milk along with the double cream and rosewater, stirring thoroughly, so that the ingredients are well mixed. Pour into moulds – cone-shaped metal moulds are traditional – and freeze until solid. Transfer to the refrigerator 20 minutes before serving, then turn out and serve.

Serves 8
Preparation time: *1 hour*, plus freezing time
Cooking time: *40 minutes*

Index

Acknowledgments

Photo Credits
Jean Cazals: front cover
Graham Kirk: back cover

Special photography by Graham Kirk

All other photos:
Octopus Publishing Group Ltd. / Jean Cazals, Jeremy Hopley, Graham Kirk,
James Murphy, Peter Myers.

Home economist
Sunil Vijayakar